☑ **W9-BEV-150**

Passport's Illustrated Travel Guide to

EGYPT

FROM
**THOMAS
COOK**

PASSPORT BOOKS
a division of *NTC Publishing Group*
Lincolnwood, Illinois USA

Published by Passport Books,
a division of NTC Publishing Group,
4255 W. Touhy Avenue,
Lincolnwood (Chicago), Illinois
60646–1975 U.S.A.

Written by Michael Haag

Original photography by Rick Strange

Edited, designed and produced by AA
Publishing.

Maps © The Automobile Association 1994, 1997

The contents of this publication are believed correct at the time of
printing. Nevertheless, the publishers cannot be held responsible for
any errors or omissions or for changes in the details given in this guide
or for the consequences of any reliance on the information provided by
the same. Assessments of attractions, hotels, restaurants, and so forth
are based upon the author's own experience and, therefore, descriptions
given in this guide necessarily contain an element of subjective opinion
that may not reflect the publishers' opinions or dictate a reader's own
experiences on another occasion.
**We have tried to ensure accuracy in this guide, but things do
change and we would be grateful if readers would advise us of
any inaccuracies they may encounter.**

Library of Congress Catalog Card Number: 96-70702

ISBN 0-8442-4835-5

Published by Passport Books in conjunction with AA Publishing and
the Thomas Cook Group Ltd.

Color separation: BTB Colour Reproduction, Whitchurch, Hampshire,
England.

Printed by Edicoes ASA, Oporto, Portugal.

Contents

About this Book

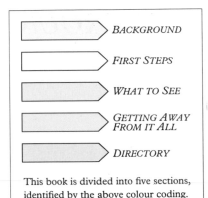

BACKGROUND

FIRST STEPS

WHAT TO SEE

GETTING AWAY FROM IT ALL

DIRECTORY

This book is divided into five sections, identified by the above colour coding.

Background gives an introduction to the country – its history, geography, politics and culture.

First Steps offers practical advice on arriving and getting around.
What to See is an alphabetical listing of places to visit, interspersed with walks and tours.
Getting Away From it All highlights places off the beaten track where it's possible to relax and enjoy the peace and quiet.
Finally, the *Directory* provides practical information – from shopping and entertainment to children and sport, including a section on business matters.
Special highly illustrated **features** on specific aspects of the country appear throughout the book.

Pyramids of Mycerinus, Chephren and Cheops

BACKGROUND

'About Egypt I shall have a great deal more to
relate because of the number of remarkable things
which the country contains, and because of the
fact that more monuments which beggar
description are
to be found there than anywhere in the world.'

HERODOTUS,
The Histories, c430BC

Introduction

*P*ervaded with an impressive sense of permanence and duration, Egypt is an eternal amalgam of two things: the constancy of the Nile and the labours of its people. Five thousand years of history have been fashioned from these elements. Like the gigantic bird migrations that sweep up the valley, storming foreigners – Persian, Greek, Arab, Turkish, British – have passed across Egypt in magnificent spectacle, but in their wake the country has remained essentially unchanged. Egyptians are warm, friendly and generous, ambitious, intelligent, religious and proud. Above all they are open and sometimes importunate so that the first-time visitor is likely to be confused, his reactions and emotions swinging like a pendulum. Yet if you can take the pace, the sheer vitality of the Egyptian people becomes a wonderful roller-coaster ride, guaranteed to brighten your visit.

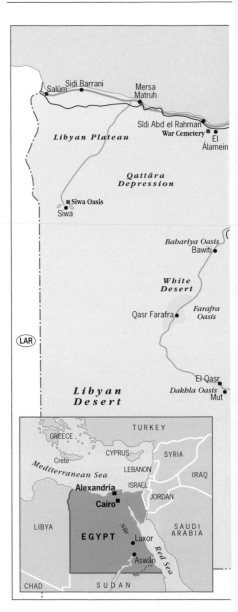

EGYPT

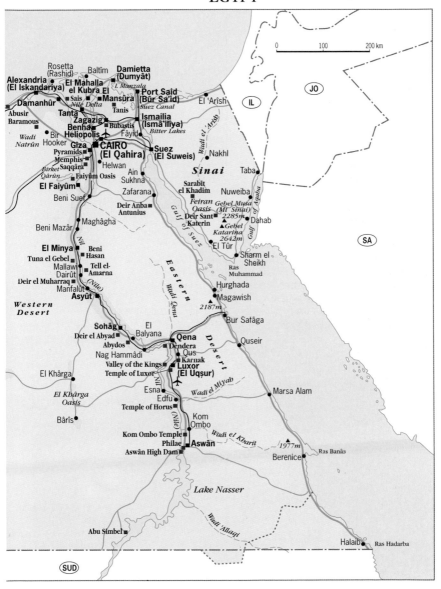

Geography

*C*overing a total area of 1,002,000sq km, Egypt occupies the extreme north-east corner of the African continent, and the Sinai peninsula, which is in Asia. It is bounded to the west by Libya, to the south by Sudan, to the east by the Red Sea and Israel, and to the north by the Mediterranean.

Central and southern Sinai is mountainous, its peaks generally ranging from 750m to 1,500m high, though Gebel Musa (Mount Sinai) rises to 2,285m and the summit of Gebel Katarina, the highest mountain in Egypt, is 2,642m. The mountain range running down Egypt's Red Sea coast is between 350m and 750m high. Otherwise Egypt is a low, flat country, the Western Desert averaging 200m above sea level, while the Nile falls only 87m in its journey of some 1,000km from Aswân to the sea. North of Cairo the river divides in two, its arms passing through the Delta and debouching into the Mediterranean at Rashid (Rosetta) and Dumyât (Damietta).

About 10,000 years ago a dramatic change in climate caused the once fertile lands of northern Africa and the Middle East to turn to dust, and their inhabitants migrated to the few remaining rivers. The Nile provided water and its annual flood covered the valley with rich alluvial soil. But the river had to be regulated, swamps drained, canals dug, fields planted and irrigated, the entire complex system maintained. To this task Egypt's peasants, the *fellahin,* gave their ceaseless labour and the state provided direction.

Sinai's mountainous peaks

Upper and Lower Egypt

Though it sometimes confuses the modern traveller to find Upper Egypt at the bottom of the map and Lower Egypt at the top, the confusion is eliminated when you remember that Memphis, the ancient capital just south of present-day Cairo, was deliberately sited to exercise a united authority over the upriver valley land (Upper Egypt) and the downriver Delta land (Lower Egypt).

The ancient Egyptians felicitously likened their united land to a lotus plant. The river valley was the stem, the Faiyûm the bud, the Delta the flower. Yet this slender figure of fertility covers less than 10 per cent of modern Egypt's total area, and within it lives 95 per cent of the nation's population, its density one of the highest in the world. The rest of the country is desert, where only a few Bedouin and oasis-dwellers can survive.

Apart from its Mediterranean coastline, where Alexandria enjoys an annual rainfall of 184mm, Egypt is exceptionally arid. Cairo receives only 24mm of rain a year, while the rest of the country receives less than 10mm. Without the Nile there could be no agriculture in Egypt.

The Nile

Until the completion of the High Dam at Aswân in 1971, all life in Egypt depended on the annual rise and fall of the Nile. The river fell throughout the winter months, reaching its lowest level in May. In June it began to rise again, reaching its peak in September. The rising Nile, which came at precisely the driest and hottest time in the Egyptian year, was caused by spring and summer rains in the African interior. The inundation also brought with it millions

Aswân's ancient Nilometer was built to measure the rise and fall of the Nile

of tons of mineral-rich sediment.

The Nile has now been backed up behind the High Dam to create Lake Nasser. Capable of holding several times more water than Egypt's annual requirement, the lake ensures a steady year-round flow from one year to the next, and so protects the country from Africa's droughts and famines.

There are ecological drawbacks, however, including the dependence on artificial fertilisers instead of silt. Also, the ancient land of Nubia, which stretched from the First Cataract at Aswân southwards into Sudan, has vanished beneath the lake. Most of the displaced Nubians, a distinct ethnic group, have been resettled around Kom Ombo.

History I

THE ROYAL DYNASTIES OF ANCIENT EGYPT

As you will discover when visiting a museum or a site, or when reading almost anything about ancient Egypt, it is the usual practice to date pharaohs, monuments and artefacts in terms of dynasties rather than by years. The system began with the ancient priests and has been adopted by Egyptologists. Additionally, Egyptologists – though not the ancient Egyptians themselves – have grouped the various dynasties into broader periods, for example Old Kingdom and New Kingdom.

The priests drew up long lists of monarchs, attaching to the years of a pharaoh's reign the events they wished to record. An example is the list of Seti I's predecessors at Abydos. Working from such lists, Manetho, an Egyptian priest under the early Ptolemies, arranged all the rulers of Egypt from Menes to Alexander into 31 dynasties.

Egyptologists have relied on Manetho's list and have been able to confirm its essential correctness while sometimes improving upon it. The dates they have attached to the dynasties, however, are subject to varying margins of error, up to 100 years for the third millenium BC, around 10 years from 2000BC onwards.

Periods, dynasties and their dates are listed below, along with some of the more important pharaohs and events associated with them.

FIRST DYNASTIC PERIOD: 3100–2700BC.

First Dynasty: 3100–2800BC. Menes (also called Narmer) unites Upper and Lower Egypt; establishes Memphis as his capital.

Second Dynasty: 2800–2700BC.

OLD KINGDOM: 2700–2200BC. Period of stability.

Third Dynasty: 2700–2650BC. Zoser builds the Step Pyramid at Saqqâra.

Fourth Dynasty: 2650–2500BC. Cheops, Chephren and Mycerinus build their pyramids at Gîza.

Fifth Dynasty: 2500–2350BC. Unas builds his pyramid at Saqqâra.

Sixth Dynasty: 2350–2200BC.

FIRST INTERMEDIATE PERIOD: 2200–2050BC. Collapse of central authority.

Seventh and Eighth Dynasties: 2180–2155BC.

Ninth and 10th Dynasties: 2155–2055BC.

11th Dynasty: 2135–2000BC.

MIDDLE KINGDOM: 2050–1800BC. Egypt reunited. Conquest of Nubia.

12th Dynasty: 1990–1780BC. Major building works and hydrological programmes in the Faiyûm.

SECOND INTERMEDIATE PERIOD: 1800–1550BC. Collapse of central authority.

13th–17th Dynasties: 1780–1570BC. The alien Hyksos people rule in Lower Egypt from 1730–1570BC. Introduction of the chariot.

NEW KINGDOM: 1570–1090BC. Period of power, luxury and cosmopolitanism.

18th Dynasty: 1570–1305BC. Hyksos expelled; royal residence and political and religious capital established at Thebes. Grandiose building works at Thebes and Karnak.

Tuthmosis I, 1525–1495BC, initiates

burials in Valley of the Kings.

Hatshepsut, 1486–1468BC, is regent for, then co-ruler with Tuthmosis III, whom she overshadows in her lifetime. Builds magnificent mortuary temple in Theban necropolis.

Tuthmosis III, 1490–1436BC, a great military leader, lays foundation for African and Asian empire.

Amenophis III, 1398–1361BC. Apogee of New Kingdom opulence.

Amenophis IV (Akhenaton), 1369–1353BC, opposes priesthood of Amun; moves capital to Tell el Amarna; establishes worship of the Aton. His queen is Nefertiti.

Tutankhamun, 1352–1344BC. Return to the worship of Amun.

19th Dynasty: 1305–1200BC.

Seti I, 1302–1290BC, revives Old Kingdom style.

Ramses II, 1290–1224BC. Prodigious builder, for example the Ramesseum and Abu Simbel.

20th Dynasty: 1200–1090BC. Egypt enters the Iron Age.

Ramses III, 1195–1164BC, defeats Sea Peoples; he is the last great pharaoh.

LATE DYNASTIC PERIOD:
1090–332BC. Period of decline; often foreign rule.

21st Dynasty: 1090–945BC. Capital at Tanis.

22nd Dynasty: 945–745BC. Libyan origin; capital at Tanis.

23rd Dynasty: 745–718BC. Ethiopian kings control Upper Egypt.

24th Dynasty: 718–712BC. Ethiopian kings control the whole of Egypt.

25th Dynasty: 712–663BC. Taharka, an Ethiopian king, builds First Pylon at Karnak; he is defeated by Assyrians who sack Thebes.

26th Dynasty: 663–525BC. Delta rulers, their capital at Sais; Assyrians

Relief carving and painting in the Temple of Seti I and Ramses II at Abydos

ejected with Greek help.

Necho, 610–595BC, attempts to link Red Sea and Mediterranean by canal. Circumnavigation of Africa.

27th Dynasty: 525–404BC. Persian rule.

28th Dynasty: 404–399BC. Persians ejected with Greek help.

29th Dynasty: 399–380BC. Delta remains centre of power.

30th Dynasty: 380–343BC.

Nectanebos I, 380–343BC, builds at Philae.

31st Dynasty: 343–332BC. Persian rule. Alexander the Great makes Egypt part of his empire in 332BC.

History II

*T*he history of ancient Egypt from its unification by Menes in about 3100BC to its conquest by Alexander the Great in 332BC is outlined on pages 10–11.

323–282BC: *Ptolemy I Soter*, one of Alexander's leading generals, makes himself king of Egypt and establishes the Ptolemaic dynasty that rules the country to the death of Cleopatra in 30BC. He founds the Mouseion with its Library at Alexandria, which, like the Ptolemies themselves, is Greek in culture. Upriver, the Ptolemies preserve the old-style pharaonic architecture and religion.
282–246BC: *Ptolemy II Philadelphos* builds the Pharos in Alexandria.
246–221BC: *Ptolemy III Euergetes* builds at Karnak; begins temple of Edfu.
221–205BC: *Ptolemy IV Philopator* begins temples at Esna and Kom Ombo.

Wall painting in Serenput II's tomb

80–51BC: *Ptolemy XII Neos Dionysos* staves off Roman annexation. Builds at Dendera, Edfu and Philae.
51–30BC: *Cleopatra VII*. Her policy is to preserve Egyptian power by joining forces with Rome. Through Julius Caesar, and then Mark Antony, she nearly succeeds.
30BC: Octavian (later Augustus Caesar) captures Alexandria. Cleopatra and Antony commit suicide; Egypt becomes a Roman province.
AD45: St Mark introduces Christianity to Egypt, according to legend.
249–251: Reign of Decius; severe Christian persecutions.
251–356: Life of St Antony, the world's first hermit.
284–305: Reign of Diocletian. His accession marks the beginning of the 'Era of Martyrs', the persecutions from which the Copts date their calendar.
313: Edict of Milan, tolerating Christianity.
About 330: Founding of the world's first monasteries, at Wadi Natrûn.
379–395: Reign of Theodosius I. He declares Christianity the official religion of the Roman Empire, which is now partitioned. Egypt is ruled from Constantinople, capital of the East Roman (Byzantine) Empire.
451: Council of Chalcedon declares the monophysite Egyptian (Coptic) Church heretical.
476: Fall of the Roman Empire in the West.
622: Móhammed's flight from Mecca, the *hegira*, from which the Muslim

calendar is reckoned.

640: Arab invasion of Egypt. Babylon (Old Cairo) falls in 641; Alexandria surrenders in 642.

878: Ibn Tulun, Abbassid governor of Egypt, makes himself independent of the Abbassid caliphate at Baghdad.

969: Cairo founded by Fatimids who invade Egypt from North Africa.

971: El Azhar founded.

1099: Crusaders take Jerusalem.

1171: Saladin founds his Ayyubid dynasty in Egypt; fortifies the Citadel. He recaptures Jerusalem in 1187.

1250–1517: Egypt ruled by Mameluke sultans, whose great builders include Qalaun (1279–90), Hassan (1347–61), Qaytbay (1469–95) and El Ghuri (1500–16).

Early 1300s: Severe persecution of the Copts, still half the population of Egypt; mass conversions to Islam follow.

1517: Egypt becomes part of the Ottoman Empire.

1798–1801: French occupation.

1805–49: Mohammed Ali makes himself master of Egypt. Begins modernisation, refounds Alexandria and establishes dynasty which lasts until Nasser's revolution.

1869: Opening of the Suez Canal.

1882: Nationalist uprising against Turkish and European influence. British occupy Egypt.

1936: Anglo-Egyptian Treaty, formally ending British occupation of Egypt, except for Canal Zone.

1939–45: British army re-enters Egypt to repel Italians and Germans. Rommel defeated at El Alamein in 1942.

1948: British leave Palestine; creation of state of Israel. Arab-Israeli war; Arab débâcle.

1952: Army officers led by Nasser stage coup; King Farouk abdicates.

Roman pillar at Babylon, Old Cairo

1956: Nasser nationalises the Suez Canal; Israel, France and Britain invade Egypt, but withdraw after international protest.

1967: Israel attacks and defeats Egypt in the 'Six Day War', and occupies Sinai.

1970: Nasser dies; Sadat becomes president.

1971: Completion of the Aswân High Dam.

1973: October War; Egyptian army crosses the canal.

1977: Sadat visits Jerusalem in dramatic peace bid.

1981: Sadat assassinated by Muslim fundamentalists. Hosni Mubarak becomes president.

1982: Israel evacuates Sinai.

1984–96: Political and economic liberalisation, but also a rise in Islamic conservatism.

Politics

*T*he United Arab Republic, to give Egypt its official title, has its capital at Cairo. Its chief executive is the president, who is elected for a six-year term. He determines the country's policies, is head of the armed forces, and he nominates the vice-president, the prime minister and other high political, civil and military officials.

The Consultative Assembly has no legislative powers. These are exercised by the People's Assembly, its members elected for a five-year term by universal suffrage. The constitution guarantees freedom of religion and thought, declares Islam to be the official religion of the state, and announces that the principles of Islamic law (*Sharia*) constitute the inspiring fount of legislation.

In the pyramid of the Egyptian state, however, the summit imposes itself on the base. There is freedom of the press, but it is undermined by sycophancy; elections take place under laws biased in favour of the ruling National Democratic Party.

Nasser's legacy
The country is still burdened by Nasser's legacy. Whatever his nationalist ideals, he was a dictator whose socialist policies helped wreck the economy.

Until recently, the population had depended more on subsidies than on opportunities. Before the deposition of King Farouk in 1952, education accounted for more than 12 per cent of government spending, while defence absorbed under 10 per cent. Defence now eats 30 per cent while education receives only six per cent. Pre-revolutionary Egypt was self-sufficient in food and its foreign exchange reserves were $25 billion in today's terms. Now it must import at least half its food, it has a national debt of over $30 billion, and were it not for foreign aid – Egypt is the second-largest recipient of American aid – the economy would collapse.

There have been some improvements. Most households now have television where few had even electricity before the revolution. Diet has improved along with working conditions for many. Infant mortality has been sharply reduced and literacy has doubled, though illiteracy is still high at 40 per cent. There are 20 times as many cars.

Nevertheless, the yawning gap between rich and poor remains. Under the monarchy the 2,000 richest people owned as much land as the 1.5 million poorest peasants. Now 70,000 Egyptians own Mercedes cars, each one worth the lifetime salary of a factory worker.

Egypt's Parliamentary Assembly in Cairo

THOMAS COOK'S EGYPT

Egypt is the country most closely associated with the history of Thomas Cook and his travel company. Cook was invited to the opening of the Suez Canal in 1869 and opened an office in Cairo. He was nearly drowned on his first Nile excursion, but survived to become owner of a fleet of 40 Nile cruisers. As the sole agent for mail and passenger traffic in Egypt, he was largely responsible for creating the booming tourist trade the country knows today. In 1884, when General Gordon was besieged by the Mahdi in Khartoum, Cook was asked to provide the transport for an Anglo-Egyptian force of 30,000 men and 100,000 tons of stores.

❖❖

President Gamal Abdel Nasser dominated Egypt until his death in 1970

Recent developments

After the revolution in 1952, nearly a quarter of a million foreigners, most of them highly skilled, were forced to leave. In recent years three million Egyptians have followed in their footsteps, seeking opportunities in the Gulf and the West.

A real effort is being made to renovate the once-beautiful cities of Cairo and Alexandria, but stretches of the north and Red Sea coasts have fallen victim to unplanned growth. Attention is being paid to newer developments such as Sharm El Sheikh to avoid similiar mistakes.

The political failures since 1952 have blocked an effective response to Egypt's greatest problem, its rocketing birth rate.

The population now stands at about 60 million, and increases by one million every nine months, outstripping land reclamation, the multiplication of harvests and the creation of new jobs. The need for birth control apart, the government has belatedly lifted the costly burden of subsidies while increasing productivity by encouraging private enterprise. Sudden reforms, however, could further impoverish the poor and cause massive job losses and political unrest. Anxiety and discontent are exploited by Islamic fundamentalists.

Yet with ample resources of water and land, with oil, an ideal location for trade, a large and cheap workforce, private capital, unparalleled tourist attractions and a high degree of social cohesion, the country also enjoys considerable advantages. Provided these are not again abused, Egypt has a future.

ISLAM

The principal belief of Islam is the existence of one God, the same God worshipped by Jews and Christians, known to all Arabs as Allah. Islam means submission. Muslim means one who submits to monotheism as interpreted by the Prophet Mohammed. Nearly 90 per cent of the Egyptian population is Muslim.

Mohammed was a merchant in Arabia. He often went to contemplate in the desert, and at the age of 40 he had a vision of the Angel Gabriel who commanded him to proclaim monotheism to the pagan Arabian tribes. He did so, and the words of Allah as given to Mohammed became known as the Koran. Concerned by the unsettling effects of this new religion, the merchants of Mecca drove Mohammed out of the city in 622. His flight (the *hegira*) from Mecca to Medina, where Islam first took root, marks the start of the Islamic calendar.

In Islam, the worshipper approaches God directly and simply. All Muslims must perform five practical devotions, the five Pillars of Faith. They must pronounce publicly that 'I bear witness that there is no god but Allah and Mohammed is his prophet'; pray five times a day; pay a tithe; fast during the month of Ramadan; and make the pilgrimage (*hadj*) to Mecca.

The most visible of these devotions is prayer. A muezzin makes the call to prayer, usually by loudspeaker these days, from the minaret of a mosque. Prayer may take place in a mosque, at home, at the office or anywhere, but worshippers always prostrate themselves in the direction of Mecca.

Westerners will be struck by the extent to which Islam permeates all areas of public and private life. This follows from the Koran, which is as much a book of laws and rules of conduct as it is a spiritual guide. Indeed, within Islam, there is no separation of the secular and religious spheres.

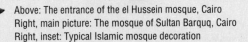

Above: The entrance of the el Hussein mosque, Cairo
Right, main picture: The mosque of Sultan Barquq, Cairo
Right, inset: Typical Islamic mosque decoration

Culture

*E*gyptian culture is Arabic, with something of an African feel. In Alexandria especially, and to a lesser extent in Cairo, there is additionally an atmosphere of the Levant, that amalgam of French, Greek, Turkish and Syrian cultures.

Following the 7th-century AD Arab invasion, the new holders of power and patrons of culture spread the Arabic language and the Islamic religion, which, with its prohibition of images, had a decisive effect in separating the greater part of Egypt's population from its pharaonic and Graeco-Roman past. That more ancient inheritance only survives in a much transmuted form within the Coptic Church.

The outlook and lifestyle of Egypt's urban middle class is not dissimilar to that of people living in Europe and America. In Cairo, for example, with its many bookshops and cinemas, its new Opera House, its cultural societies and universities, there is ample opportunity to share in and contribute to the broad international experience.

Life is a grind for the poorer inhabitants of the cities, though many willingly seek its slender promise rather than endure the monotonous labour of the countryside, which has gone largely unchanged since pharaonic times. Relief is provided by television and the cinema, but also by such popular celebrations as *moulids,* the Egyptian equivalent of medieval European saints' fairs. Here booths sell crafts and sweets, here marriages are arranged. There is music, the chanting of dervishes, puppet shows and story-tellers, songs and dancing.

The novels of Naguib Mahfouz, who won the Nobel Prize in 1989, offer a vivid portrait of modern Egypt throughout all ranges of its society.

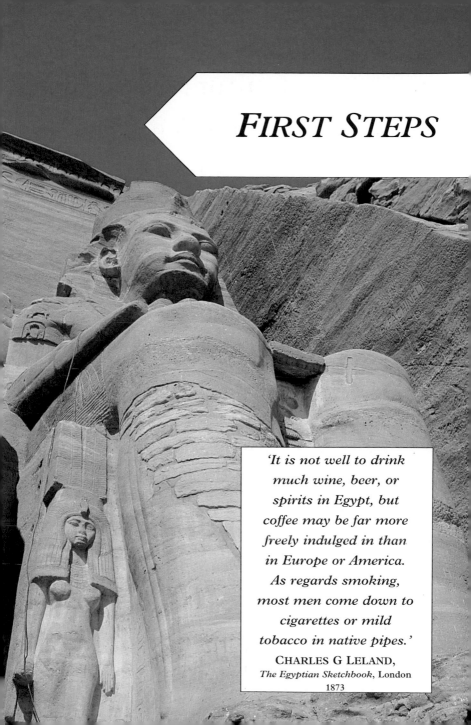

FIRST STEPS

'It is not well to drink much wine, beer, or spirits in Egypt, but coffee may be far more freely indulged in than in Europe or America. As regards smoking, most men come down to cigarettes or mild tobacco in native pipes.'

CHARLES G LELAND,
The Egyptian Sketchbook, London
1873

FIRST IMPRESSIONS

Arriving in Egypt is like entering a bazaar. Your senses are invaded with its colour, its noise, its smells, its animation. Movement is eager, heaving, seemingly chaotic. Everything is thrust at you.

Well, Egypt *is* something of a bazaar, and it is up to you how much you want to respond to what is on offer. At first you may feel overwhelmed and uncertain, but you are free to browse. Nobody will mind if you take your time in getting the measure of the place.

Arabic

The language of Egypt is Arabic. It is written from right to left, using an alphabet of 29 letters. There is no completely satisfactory system for conveying the sound of Arabic letters in Western languages. Nor is there agreement on the transliteration of Egyptian place-names. Therefore Faiyûm might appear as Fayyum, Saqqâra as Sakkara, Dendera as Dendarah and so on. This can present an even bigger problem when it is the initial letters that vary, for example Edfu instead of Idfu, or Qena instead of Kena. So do not rely entirely on spelling; instead try to think phonetically when looking for places on maps, signs and in this guide.

For the sake of simplicity, *El* (or *el*) has been used throughout this guide, for example El Azhar rather than Al Azhar (or al-Azhar). The Arabic for street is *sharia,* and for square it is *midan* – or at least those are the spellings used here. These come before the name, for example Sharia Ramses and Midan el Tahrir.

Baksheesh

The word *baksheesh* literally means 'share the wealth'. It is payable for all services, however small, and, as often as not, is expected for nothing at all. Alms-giving is a central tenet of Islam, and few Egyptians will balk at accepting their share. You have it, they do not, and so they feel you should pass it round.

Baksheesh is the tip you might give to the man who has carried your luggage. It is also the reward placed deftly in the outstretched hand of the guardian who lets you into a tomb after closing time, or given to the railway carriage attendant who discovers there *is* a sleeping compartment free after all.

There may be times when you wish to give something out of charity – that, too, is *baksheesh.* But *baksheesh* can be a plague. Children may pester you for it in the streets, or you may have paid but are pressed for more. The basic rule is to offer *baksheesh* only in return for a service, not to pay until the service has been performed, and to resist firmly any intimidation.

Catching cold

When you think of Egypt you think of sun and heat, and so you will, of course, think of taking light clothes, sunglasses and a hat or scarf to protect yourself against sunstroke. But that is not the whole of the story.

You need to be aware of the extremes of temperature in Egypt, and that can mean extremes of cold as well as heat. The desert can be punishingly hot by day but it can rapidly become chilly, and outside the summer months cold, as soon as the sun goes down. Even attending the sound and light show at the Gîza Pyramids on the edge of the desert can prove uncomfortably cool.

The same is true of the mountainous landscapes of Sinai and along the Red Sea coast – you could easily turn blue on top of Mount Sinai while waiting for the sun to rise. In the desert and the mountains you should carry a sweater with you at night, even in summer. For details of climate, see page 178.

Smoking a *nargileh* or *shisha*

READING THE SIGNS

The Arabic alphabet is completely different to that of other languages, but in general, street signs and all other notices relevant to the tourist will be written in English, or sometimes French. You may soon come to recognise one word, however, which you will frequently see not only in mosques but on the walls of shops, restaurants, almost anywhere – the Arabic for Allah:

You should make an effort to learn the Arabic numerals (from which Western numerals have derived). This will help you identify numbered buses and railway carriages, and understand prices.

HIEROGLYPHS

Hieroglyphs began in around 3000BC as picture writing, that is the pictures conveyed an idea or story. Soon a phonetic alphabet of 24 letters was introduced, and if only these had been used then reading hieroglyphs would be easy. Additionally, however, the priests used more than 700 signs representing syllables. There are books available explaining how to read the more common symbols. A distinctive feature of hieroglyphs is the cartouche, a stylised loop of rope which always encloses the name of a ruler, thereby conveying the idea of unending, unbroken, unchanging power.

In the 1820s, Jean François Champollion guessed that cartouches enclosed the names of rulers. When he saw a number of cartouches on the Rosetta Stone, then saw repeated below these in Greek the names of several rulers, he was able to match Greek letters to hieroglyphic symbols (see page 128).

K   L   I   O   P   A   D   R   A

NUMERALS

١	٢	٣	٤	٥	٦	٧	٨	٩	١٠
1	2	3	4	5	6	7	8	9	10

THE CROWN

Pharaohs are always shown wearing a crown, either the White Crown of Upper Egypt or the Red Crown of Lower Egypt. Frequently, the two are combined, representing the pharaoh's authority over a united Egypt. At the front of the pharaonic crown is the *uraeus,* a hooded cobra, to ward off his enemies.

WHITE (Upper Egypt)

RED (Lower Egypt)

COMBINED
(Unified Kingdom)

Right: Relief carving in the Temple of Hathor, Philae, showing an example of the combined crown of Egypt

Inshallah, bukra and *maalesh*

Part of Egyptian tradition, though increasingly out of date in today's faster-moving Egypt, are three commonly heard words, *inshallah, bukra* and *maalesh,* whose meaning, and more importantly whose nuance, you should know. Together they provide some insight into how things work, or frequently do not work, in Egypt.

Inshallah means 'God willing', and, reasonably enough, it conveys the caution that even with the best of human intentions nothing can be certain. However, it can also be a polite way of avoiding a commitment, indeed of suggesting that the thing promised will not happen.

Bukra means 'tomorrow', but it would be a mistake to take this literally. *Bukra,* in fact, more usually refers to some indefinite point in time between tomorrow and never.

Maalesh means it does not matter anyway.

Living standards

The living standards of a great number of Egyptians are very low, and visitors may be distressed at the poverty they will sometimes encounter. Egyptians, however, are a proud people. Family and neighbourhood networks serve as a form of social security system. There is no homelessness here. Numerous people may pack into a room or families may live among the tombs in Cairo's City of the Dead, but no one sleeps out on the street. Outright begging is extremely rare; the request for *baksheesh* usually supposes that some service has been performed. Your greatest contribution to the situation is simply visiting Egypt – directly and indirectly, tourism creates jobs.

Manners and customs

Egyptian values are rooted in the strong family attachments of a still overwhelmingly rural heritage and in Islam's closely woven social code. Though allowances are made for foreign idiosyncrasies, the same conservative behaviour and dress is expected of you.

Physicality should be muted, so that men and women should refrain from kissing and hugging in public, while generally, it is a good idea not to show too much flesh. Except at resorts intended for Westerners, no one, especially women, should wear shorts. Skirts and dresses should fall below the knee, and both women and men should cover their shoulders.

Do not photograph an Egyptian without asking permission. For some people it is extremely offensive, while others, who might not have minded, will feel that you have taken a liberty. If you do ask first, people are often happy to be photographed, and indeed the occasion can be a way of getting to know people. Egyptians can be sensitive about many scenes you might find picturesque but which to them portray poverty or backwardness. If someone asks you to desist, it is best to do so and look for another chance elsewhere. Militarily sensitive subjects – including airports, railway stations, dams, bridges and government offices – should not be photographed.

During the month of Ramadan, Muslims may not eat, drink or smoke while the sun is up. It would be polite if you, too, refrained, in public at least.

If you are invited to someone's home, it is customary to bring a gift, such as sweet pastries.

Right: the Eye of Horus on a felucca

SUPERSTITION

Superstition says that the envious glance of a passer-by, attracted by an immodest show of wealth, achievement or beauty, can harm or bewitch. Reciting certain verses of the Koran is one way of warding it off; the Eye of Horus is another commonly used. It may be painted on cars, trucks and fishing boats, or worn as an amulet, particularly by children, who are especially vulnerable to the 'evil eye'. Therefore, it is a good idea not to admire something too much – your behaviour can be mistaken for covetousness, and you may find that you are given it.

Moustache

You do not actually need to have a moustache to be called one. 'Moustache', or more formally 'Mister Moustache', is what Egyptians, usually touts, sometimes call male foreigners. More generally the foreigner, male or female, is called a *khawaga*, which also conveys the sense that you have lots of money which you are about to share (see **Baksheesh**, page 20).

Security

Egypt is a safe country for visitors. You are far safer walking through the streets of Cairo, where muggings are unheard of, than through those of many European or American cities – and that is true both day and night.

There is a strong sense of communal responsibility, especially towards foreigners. Anyone in distress can expect the immediate assistance of both public and police.

Egyptian police in summer uniform

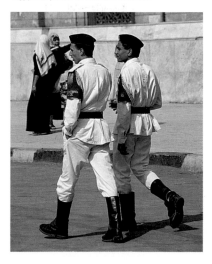

In addition to the regular Metropolitan Police, who wear black uniforms in winter, white uniforms in summer, and who mostly speak only Arabic, there are special police who wear the same uniform but with a red armband saying 'Tourist Police'. They all speak a foreign language, usually English (not necessarily fluently, however), and are posted at tourist sights, museums, airports, railway stations and ports. They are there to help if you are experiencing difficulties.

There are also the more soldierly-looking Central Security Police, always dressed in black and armed with automatic weapons, who guard embassies, banks and other public buildings.

A few fundamentalist fanatics who would like to turn Egypt into a theocratic Islamic state have been attempting to attack the government, and indeed the economy of the country, through tourism. By threatening and frightening away foreign visitors, their hope has been to destroy a major source of Egypt's income. Egyptians are overwhelmingly opposed to such outrages and the government has responded with determination, but as in London or New York it is never entirely possible to guarantee the elimination of terrorist activity. What can be said is that Egyptians remain a warm, good-humoured and hospitable people who care about the welfare of visitors to their country.

Touts

Touts are most common and relentless at the obvious tourist places, like the Pyramids at Gîza, or along the corniche at Luxor. A polite but firm *la shukran*, ('no thank you'), should be enough to

turn away unwanted attentions. If forced to rudeness, then *imshee*, ('get lost'), has the almost physical effect of a slap in the face.

Do not assume that everyone is out to take advantage of you. People are often simply curious, or wish to be helpful.

Visiting mosques and monasteries
In visiting Islamic mosques and Christian monasteries, you are entering into the most conservative areas of Egyptian life and therefore should take special care to dress and act with decorum. Neither shorts nor short skirts should be worn, nor should shoulders be bare. Inside mosques you must remove your shoes, or shoe coverings will be

Shoe rack outside a mosque – you must remove your footwear before entering

provided. For this, or if you accept the services of a guide, or ask to be shown the way up a minaret, *baksheesh* will be expected in addition to any entry fee.

You may sometimes find yourself in a mosque at prayer time. Then, though visitors are otherwise welcome, you may be asked to retreat into an alcove or out on to the street.

Except for St Catherine's Monastery in Sinai, which is Greek Orthodox, all Egyptian monasteries are Coptic. The Copts go in for a good deal of fasting, and during such periods their monasteries are closed to visitors. For further details, see page 179.

Women travellers

Westerners going to Egypt are, to some extent, putting themselves in a position of contrast to the conventions of social life there. This is especially true in the case of Western women.

An Egyptian woman's life is very much bound up, indeed bounded, by her family relationships, whether as daughter, wife or mother. The entwined moral, religious and legal systems of the country enforce this. Even an educated woman would be most circumspect in her relationship with a man; both families would be involved and meetings limited to public situations.

Your Western view may be that that is their business and your business is your own. Some Egyptians will make the effort to see it that way, especially as you are only passing through. A great many more will not agree.

Things are changing in Egypt, however. In Cairo and other cosmopolitan places, many Egyptian women dress in the same styles as their Western counterparts. If in doubt, especially in less tourist-exposed areas, dress conservatively.

A woman walking about or travelling on her own may be pestered but, as in other countries, it depends on how she chooses to dress and how she reacts. You can reduce the chances of being hassled by dressing and behaving conservatively. If it helps, wear a wedding ring. Or keep in the company of other women, including Egyptian women, for example when travelling on a train. Egyptian women will happily adopt you into their circle.

There is no reason for you to put up with unwelcome attention. If, at worst, you are touched up, you can first say *imshee,* which means 'get lost'. If something stronger is called for, shout *sibnee le wahadee,* which means 'don't touch me'. People will come to your aid and the man will be thoroughly ashamed, probably on the run.

WHAT TO SEE

'You can never in your thoughts detach the Egypt of the past from the Egypt of today; neither, indeed, can you ever quite exclude it from sight.'

HOWARD HOPLEY,
Under Egyptian Palms,
London 1869

Cairo

*C*airo is not only the largest city in Africa but also the political and cultural pivot of the Arab world. Its population of around 15 million has grown five-fold within a generation as *fellahin* (Egypt's peasantry) have poured in from the countryside in search of opportunities. New bridges, flyovers and an excellent metro system keep the city from grinding to a halt, and there is constant new building.

The most modern part of the city lies close to the Nile, which breathes through Cairo like a giant lung. Further east, towards the Moqattam Hills, is the medieval city of splendid mosques and thronging bazaars, founded by the Fatimids in AD969. To the south is the now ruinous Fustat, the earliest Arab settlement, built when they invaded Egypt around AD641. Westwards, beyond the sprawl of Gîza, the Pyramids glow gold at sundown against the Western Desert as they have done for 1,700,000 evenings past.

ABU SARGA CHURCH
(St Sargius)
See page 43.
Old Cairo (Misr el Qadima). 4.5km south of Midan el Tahrir. Open: 8am–4pm. Free. Metro: Mari Girgis.

AQUEDUCT
Much of the 3.5km-long Mameluke aqueduct (1311–1505), which once brought water from the Nile to the Citadel, still survives. It is most easily seen opposite the midpoint of Roda Island.

EL AZHAR MOSQUE
The El Azhar ('the most blooming') was completed in AD971, the first mosque built by the Fatimids in their new city of Cairo. The world's foremost centre of Islamic theological teaching, it is also the oldest university in the world, with modern schools of medicine, science and languages near by.

Although much rebuilt in a confusion of styles, the overall impression is of harmony, the atmosphere venerable. In deep arcades off the central court, theological teachers sit at the bases of columns, surrounded by their students, as was done a thousand years ago. There are wonderful views of the medieval city from the roof and minarets.
Sharia el Azhar. 3km east of Midan el Tahrir. Open: 9am–3pm. Closed: 11am–1pm during Friday prayers. Admission charge.

Nearby
Khan el Khalili (see pages 35 and 41).

BAB ZUWAYLA, BAB EL FUTUH AND BAB EL NASR
The three surviving gates to the Fatimid city. (See pages 40–1.)

BAYT EL SUHAYMI
This merchant's house of the Ottoman period, built during the 16th and 17th centuries, and completely furnished to the age, is the finest house in Cairo and a wonderful example of Islamic secular architecture – which strives towards paradise. Beautifully decorated rooms include the men's dining loggia, and the

CENTRAL CAIRO

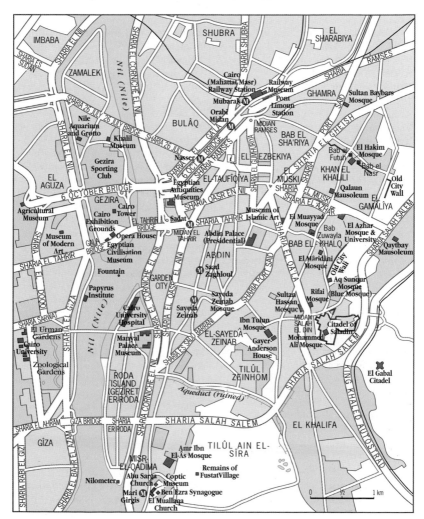

women's *harem*, with its own private chapel and bath-house, and bedrooms screened with intricately patterned *mashrabiyya* windows. Arranged around a garden courtyard, the dwelling is always deliciously cool. (See page 41.)

Haret el Darb el Asfar, east of Sharia el Muizz. 3km east of Midan el Tahrir. Open: 9am–4pm. Admission charge.

BEN EZRA SYNAGOGUE

See page 43.
Old Cairo (Misr el Qadima). 4.5km south of Midan el Tahrir. Open: 8am–4pm. Free. Metro: Mari Girgis.

CAIRO TOWER

Rising like a giant lotus 187m above the island of Gezira, the tower's open observation platform and enclosed café and restaurant offer spectacular, panoramic views of the city.
Sharia el Burg el Qahira, towards the southern end of Gezira Island. 1km west of Midan el Tahrir. Open: 9am–midnight. Admission charge.

THE CITADEL

In 1176 Saladin built his fortress on this spur of the Moqattam Hills, which commands a watchful view of the whole of Cairo. For almost 700 years, to the death of Mohammed Ali in 1849, nearly all Egypt's rulers lived in the Citadel, held court, dispensed justice and received ambassadors. (See page 39.)

THE CITADEL

The Citadel overlooks Midan Salah el Din, 3km southeast of Midan el Tahrir. Open: 9am–4pm. Closed: Friday 11.30am–1pm. General admission charge. The Carriage and Military Museums are extra.

Bijou Palace

Mohammed Ali's palace, with its French-style salons, is now a museum of 19th-century royal portraits, costumes and furnishings.

Citadel Museums

The **Carriage Museum** contains six royal carriages, including one of gold. The **Military Museum** is filled less with hardware than with the ceremonial bric-à-brac of war. The **National Police Museum** includes rooms devoted to Egypt's most famous murders and assassinations, though not President Sadat's.

El Nasr Mohammed Mosque

Built during the early 14th century by the Mameluke Sultan el Nasr Mohammed, the marble panelling and much of the faïence decoration of the exterior were long ago stripped away, creating an austere impression. The arcades around the central courtyard, however, remain elegant in their proportions, their columns taken from pharaonic, Roman and Byzantine buildings.

Mohammed Ali Mosque

A Turkish delight on the Cairo skyline, the mosque was built in imitation of the Ottoman imperial mosques of Istanbul. Half domes rise as buttresses for the high central dome, while two thin minarets add an ethereal touch. Mohammed Ali's tomb is on the right as you enter the vast and opulently decorated interior (see page 35). From the courtyard outside, pollution permitting, there is a superb view of the city.

COPTIC MUSEUM

This charming building, beautifully decorated with carved beams and *mashrabiyyas,* covers the period from the late Roman Empire through the early Middle Ages when Egypt was a largely Christian country. Its collection, gathered from churches and houses, links the art of the pharaonic and Graeco-Roman periods with that of Islam. Attention is given to stonework, manuscripts, textiles, icons and paintings, woodwork, metalwork, pottery and glass. It is very much a folk art, often agreeably naive, though in textiles the Copts achieved a rare brilliance, weaving a delightful brightness and movement into their work. (See page 42.)

Old Cairo (Masr el Qadima). 4.5km south of Midan el Tahrir. Tel: 362 8766. Open: 9am–4pm. Closed: Friday 11am–1pm. Admission charge. Metro: Mari Girgis.

EGYPTIAN ANTIQUITIES MUSEUM

This is a unique storehouse of one of the oldest and grandest civilisations on earth. The arrangement is more or less chronological, so that starting at the entrance and walking clockwise round the ground floor you pass from Old Kingdom through Middle Kingdom and New Kingdom exhibits (the highlight on this floor is the Akhenaton room at the rear), concluding with Ptolemaic and Roman exhibits. The first floor contains prehistoric and early dynastic exhibits and the contents of several tombs, most notably the magnificent array of wealth from Tutankhamun's. In the Mummy Room lie the bodies of such great pharaohs as Seti I and Ramses II.

Midan el Tahrir. Tel: 5754319. Open: 9am–4pm. Closed: Friday 11.15am–1.30pm. Admission charge, plus charge for the Mummy Room. Metro: Sadat.

The Mohammed Ali Mosque, also known as the Alabaster Mosque, was built between 1830 and 1848

GAYER-ANDERSON HOUSE

Named for a British major who restored and occupied what is in fact two 17th-century houses knocked together, the house is filled with his anachronistic collection of English, French and oriental furniture and bric-à-brac which gives the place a lived-in feel. The large reception room, with its fountain and decorated ceiling, is overlooked by a balcony enclosed by a *mashrabiyya* screen through which the women of the *harem* could discreetly observe male visitors. (See page 39.)

Abuts the Ibn Tulun Mosque off Sharia el Salibah, 500m west of the Citadel. 3km southeast of Midan el Tahrir. Tel: 3647822. Open; 8.30am–4pm. Closed: Friday 11am –1.30pm. Admission charge, valid also for the Islamic Arts Museum on the same day.

EL GHURI WAKALA

This merchants' hostel and warehouse of the Mameluke period now serves as workshops for artisans and sells Bedouin crafts. (See page 41.)

Sharia Mohammed Abduh, near El Azhar Mosque. 3km east of Midan el Tahrir. Tel: 920472. Open: 9am–5pm. Closed: Friday. Admission charge.

IBN TULUN MOSQUE

One of the oldest and finest mosques in Cairo. (See page 38.)
Off Sharia el Salibah, 500m west of the Citadel. 3km southeast of Midan el Tahrir. Open: 9am–4pm. Admission charge.

ISLAMIC ART MUSEUM

Your explorations of medieval Cairo will be greatly enriched by a visit to this museum, which contains many beautiful objects from its mosques and houses. Some of the displays group fountains, furniture, *mashrabiyyas* and architectural decorations together to recreate the atmosphere of a home or place of worship. The collection is arranged in part chronologically, giving you a sense

Nargilehs for sale – bazaar scene in Cairo's Khan el Khalili

of Fatimid, Mameluke and Ottoman styles, while some rooms are devoted to woodwork, metalwork, pottery and manuscripts of all periods, and also include works of art from Turkey, Iraq, Persia, Spain and China.

Intersection of Sharias Port Said and El Qa'la. 1.5km southeast of Midan el Tahrir. Tel: 3909930. Open: 9am–4pm. Closed: Friday 11am–2pm. Admission charge, valid also for the Gayer-Anderson House on the same day.

KHAN EL KHALILI

The wealth of Cairo was built on trade, and caravans from all over Africa and Asia disgorged their cargoes for sale at the numerous bazaars that make up Khan el Khalili. Much of that medieval atmosphere still survives among the narrow covered passageways where you can join throngs of Cairenes to bargain over spices and perfume oils, gold and silver jewellery, leather goods and fabrics. (See page 41)

Within the northeast angle of Sharias el Muizz and el Muski, though spilling beyond as well. 3km east of Midan el Tahrir. Activity continues well on into the night.

MANYAL PALACE

Built in 1903 for Prince Mohammed Ali, brother of the Khedive Abbas II, this oriental, rococo-style palace, set in a garden of banyan trees on Roda Island, is worth visiting for the opulence of its decorations and for its royal mementos. Displays include a 1,000-piece silver service, a table made of elephants' ears and a stuffed hermaphrodite goat.

Sharia Ahmed Abdel Rahim, Roda Island. 2km south of Midan el Tahrir. Tel: 987495. Open: 9am–4pm. Admission charge.

MOHAMMED ALI MOSQUE

This Ottoman-style mosque dominates the skyline from the top of the Citadel. (See page 32.)

EL MUALLAQA CHURCH

This is popularly known as the Hanging Church because it is built atop the two walls of the Roman fortress. (See pages 42–3.)

Old Cairo (Masr el Qadima). 4.5km south of Midan el Tahrir. Open: 8am–4pm. Free. Metro: Mari Girgis.

NILOMETER

Dating from the 9th century the Nilometer, a graduated column, measured the rise and fall of the Nile, and was built to determine the size of harvest and what taxes should be imposed.

Southern tip of Roda Island. 4.5km south of Midan el Tahrir. Open: 9am–4pm. Closed: Friday. Admission charge.

OTHER MUSEUMS
As well as the Coptic, Islamic and Egyptian Antiquities museums, each of which is a must, and the minor museums of the Citadel (see page 32), there are several others worth visiting.

Agricultural Museum
Set within a beautiful garden of specimen trees, this is, in fact, three museums: the **Historical Museum** has displays of agricultural life in pharaonic times; the **Agricultural and Cotton Museum** concentrates on modern times, especially on Egypt's major cash crop; and the **Natural History and Ethnological Museum** covers the animal life, hydrology, rural crafts and culture of the Nile valley and Delta.
At the west end of 6 October Bridge. 2km west of Midan el Tahrir. Tel: 702933. Open: Tuesday to Sunday 9am–2pm. Closed: Monday. Admission charge.

Papyrus Institute
Designed to preserve the ancient Egyptian art of papyrus-making, the institute contains a museum displaying the stages in the process. Sheets of papyrus can be purchased.
On a houseboat docked at Giza's Corniche el Nil, near the Cairo Sheraton. 1.5km west of Midan el Tahrir. Tel: 3488676. Open: 9am–7pm. Free.

Railway Museum
This museum is for train buffs of all ages, with automated displays and old steam engines and carriages, including the Khedive Ismael's private train.
Midan Ramses, next to the main railway station. 2km northeast of Midan el Tahrir. Tel: 763793. Open: Tuesday to Sunday 8.30am–1pm. Closed: Friday noon, all day Monday. Admission charge.

The Mameluke Sultan Hassan Mosque

Modern painting on papyrus

QAYTBAY MAUSOLEUM

The Eastern Cemetery (Qarafat el Sharqiyya), as the **City of the Dead** is properly known, is the burial place of several of the greatest Mameluke sultans, among them Qaytbay, whose mausoleum, completed in 1474, is one of the finest buildings in Cairo. The exterior of the exquisitely proportioned dome is decorated with intricate reliefs of filigree flowers upon star-shaped polygons. The tomb chamber within is of immense height, its decoration breathtakingly variegated. The City of the Dead is far from being without life. The poor have always made their homes here, while relatives visit the more recent family tombs on feast days for a picnic.
East of Sharia Salah Salem. 1km east of El Azhar Mosque, 4km east of Midan el Tahrir. Open: 8am–4pm. Admission charge.

RIFAI MOSQUE

A burial place of royalty. (See page 39.)
Midan Salah el Din. 3km southeast of Midan el Tahrir. Open: 8am–4pm. Admission charge.

SITT BARBARA CHURCH

A 7th-century Coptic church containing the relics of an early martyr. (See page 43.)
Old Cairo (Masr el Qadima). 4.5km south of Midan el Tahrir. Open: 8am–4pm. Free. Metro: Mari Girgis.

THE MAMELUKES

As you walk through the streets of medieval Cairo (see pages 40–1), you can still taste the atmosphere of *The Thousand and One Nights*. The tales were set in the 9th-century Baghdad of Haroun el Rashid, but in reality they portray Cairo during the turbulence and spectacle of the Mameluke period (1250–1517).

The Mamelukes began as a slave militia, but they soon became an indispensable military elite. After overthrowing Saladin's dynasty, successive sultans rose from their number. The Mamelukes saved Egypt from the Mongols and finished the task of driving the Crusaders from the Holy Land.

Ruthless for power and often brutal, they nevertheless enriched Cairo with their bold and voluminous architecture, decorating its surfaces with intricate stalactite motifs and graceful arabesques. The mosque of Sultan Hassan and the mausoleum of Qaytbay are the two finest monuments from Mameluke times.

The last Mameluke sultan was hanged by the Ottomans at Bab Zuwayla, but they remained a power in the land until their destruction by Mohammed Ali early in the 19th century.

SULTAN HASSAN MOSQUE

The finest Mameluke mosque in Cairo and regarded by many as the outstanding Islamic monument in Egypt. (See page 39.)
Midan Salah el Din. 3km southeast of Midan el Tahrir. Open: 8am–6pm. Admission charge.

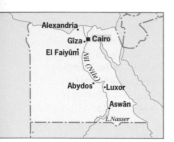

Ibn Tulun Mosque to the Citadel

This walk takes you to four famous mosques and the Gayer-Anderson House, and concludes with a sweeping view of Cairo. *Allow 3 hours.*

Begin at the Ibn Tulun Mosque.

1 IBN TULUN MOSQUE

In the 9th century, when the Arab world was ruled from Baghdad, Ibn Tulun was sent to govern Egypt. He borrowed the idea for his remarkable spiral minaret, which you can climb, from the Great Mosque of Samarra in Iraq. He also introduced the technique of carved stucco which adorns the arches around the vast central court. Designed as a congregational mosque to accommodate thousands of worshippers during Friday prayers, this is the finest example of its kind in Cairo. The impression is of severe simplicity, but you should walk round the court under the arcades to appreciate the rhythm of the arches and the play that is made with light and shadow. (See page 34.)

Abutting the southeast corner of the mosque is the Gayer-Anderson House.

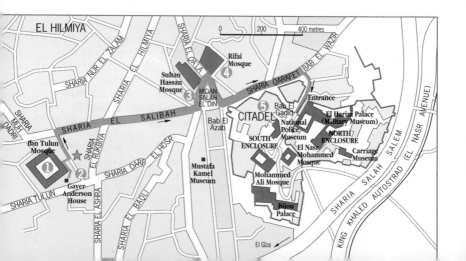

Courtyard of the Ibn Tulun Mosque

2 GAYER-ANDERSON HOUSE

See page 34.

Walk east along Sharia el Salibah to Midan Salah el Din. At its north end, two large mosques stand close together. The nearest is the Sultan Hassan Mosque.

3 SULTAN HASSAN MOSQUE

This Mameluke mosque of the 1350s was reputedly built of stone taken from the Pyramid of Cheops. Its enormous portal with stalactite decorations (a favourite Mameluke motif) leads you into a dark corridor from which you emerge into a brilliant sun-filled central court surrounded by magnificently soaring vaults, called *liwans*. Unlike the Ibn Tulun, designed to be a great gathering place, the Sultan Hassan was primarily a *madrasa* or theological school, the *liwans* serving as places of study.

You should sit here a while, contemplating the wonderful interplay of dark and light, concrete and void. Beyond the sanctuary *liwan* with its *mihrab* is Hassan's mausoleum. (See page 37.)

Cross Sharia el Qa'la to the Rifai Mosque.

4 RIFAI MOSQUE

Built early this century in mock-Mameluke style, the Rifai Mosque owes its fame to the tombs here of several members of Mohammed Ali's dynasty, including King Farouk, who was deposed in 1952. The ex-Shah of Iran is also buried here. (See page 37.)

Cross Midan Salah el Din to the base of the Citadel.

5 THE CITADEL

The western gate, Bab el Azab, is closed to the public. Here, Mohammed Ali massacred the Mamelukes in 1811, making himself absolute master of Egypt. Sent by the sultan in Istanbul to restore Ottoman authority after Napoleon's departure, his presence was resented by the Mamelukes. After inviting them to dinner at the Citadel, he locked the gate as they attempted to leave and shot them down with their bellies full.

Atop the Citadel (see page 32) is the most familiar landmark in Cairo, the Mohammed Ali Mosque, famous also for its view. Looking westwards, you can trace your walk; the Rifai and Sultan Hassan mosques down below, and further off, the great rectangle of the Ibn Tulun Mosque.

SALADIN

Salah el Din, better known in the West as Saladin, was the chivalrous adversary of Richard the Lionheart during the Crusades. Of Kurdish stock, he became the champion of orthodox Sunni Islam, putting an end to Shi'ite Fatimid rule in Egypt and, after fortifying the Citadel, taking Jerusalem from the Crusaders in 1187.

Sharia el Muizz and Khan el Khalili

This walk takes you through the heart of the medieval city, the world of *The Thousand and One Nights. Allow 3 hours.*

Nearby

1 Islamic Art Museum
(see pages 34–5)

Begin at Bab Zuwayla.

1 BAB ZUWAYLA

Until the 19th century, medieval Cairo was encircled by 60 gates, of which only three remain. Eleventh-century Bab

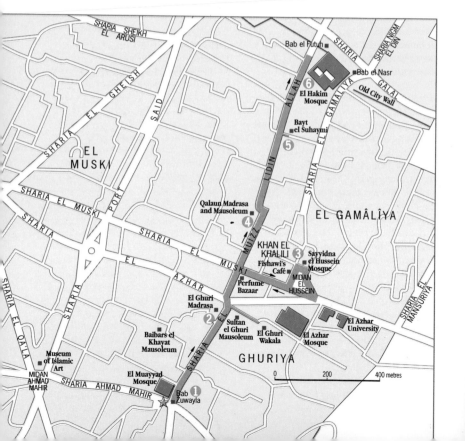

Zuwayla was the principal southern gate and the place of public executions.

Running north from the gate is Sharia el Muizz, the main street of the Fatimid city. The first building on the left is the 15th-century El Muayyad Mosque. From inside you can climb to the top of Bab Zuwayla for a fine view. *Continue north along Sharia el Muizz.*

2 EL GHURI MADRASA, MAUSOLEUM AND WAKALA

Just before the intersection with Sharia el Azhar are the red-and-white-striped *madrasa* (left) and mausoleum (right) of the 16th-century Mameluke Sultan El Ghuri. Whirling Dervishes sometimes perform at the mausoleum. At the intersection turn right. After 100m is El Ghuri's *wakala,* the best preserved example of a merchants' hostel in Cairo. (See page 34.)
Retrace your steps, cross Sharia el Azhar and continue north along Sharia el Muizz.

3 KHAN EL KHALILI

This is the Spice Bazaar, on the edge of the vast warren that is Khan el Khalili (see page 35). Turning right at the market street of Muski you come to the Perfume Bazaar. Sharia el Muski continues east into a large square overlooked to the south by the 10th-century El Azhar Mosque (see page 30) and to the north by Sayyidna el Hussein Mosque (non-Muslims not normally admitted). To the west of the square is Fishawi's, a famous café where you can refresh yourself.
From Sharia el Muski, walk 200m north along Sharia el Muizz.

4 QALAUN MADRASA AND MAUSOLEUM

On your left you see three domes, each with a stout minaret, a splendid cluster of buildings by the Mameluke sultans Qalaun, El Nasr and Barquq. The finest of these complexes is the late 13th-century work of Qalaun.

Inside, on the left, is the *madrasa* or theological school, on the right Qalaun's mausoleum, a masterpiece of Mameluke architecture, richly ornamented with wood, stucco and stone inlay beneath a soaring dome pierced by stained-glass windows.
Walk north along Sharia el Muizz, then turn right into Haret el Darb el Asfar.

5 BAYT EL SUHAYMI

See pages 30–1.
Continue north along Sharia el Muizz.

6 EL HAKIM MOSQUE

The 11th-century Fatimid Caliph el Hakim declared himself God and answered objections by chopping off heads and burning down half of Cairo. He was assassinated at the instigation of his sister. For centuries an aura of dread hung about the mosque, and it was allowed to crumble. It has now been brightly restored.

Bab Zuwayla, imposing medieval gate

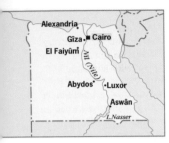

Coptic Cairo

This walk introduces you to some of the oldest churches in Egypt, as well as to its oldest synagogue. *Allow 1 hour, plus time for the museum.*

Begin at the Mari Girgis metro station, facing the towers of the Roman fortress.

1 ROMAN FORTRESS
The section of wall and two towers are part of a Roman fortress which was built around 30BC, after Augustus had defeated Antony and Cleopatra. The fortress once encompassed all the sites covered in this walk, but much of it was demolished by the British in the 19th century.

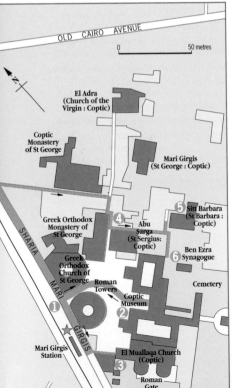

After purchasing a ticket to the Coptic Museum and passing across its inner courtyard, you can descend to the level of the Roman water gate, into which the Nile still seeps, and step along raised walkways beneath arches and vaults. Above you is El Muallaqa Church.

2 COPTIC MUSEUM
The two Roman towers also mark the entrance to the grounds of the Coptic Museum (see pages 32–3), its exhibits gathered from ancient churches and houses.
Go out between the Roman towers and turn left, following the walls round to the steps rising to the level of El Muallaqa.

3 EL MUALLAQA CHURCH
(Church of The Virgin)
This is popularly known as the Hanging Church because it is suspended on beams laid across the two bastions of the Roman water gate. It was probably built after the 7th-century Arab conquest, once the walls had become

El Muallaqa, one of the oldest places of Christian worship in Egypt

Faded paintings of the apostles, probably 8th-century, adorn the columns of the nave, while 12th-century carved wooden panels on the altar screen depict the Nativity and Last Supper. (See page 30.)

Turn right out of Abu Sarga and then right at the corner. At the end of the street you see Sitt Barbara to the left.

5 SITT BARBARA CHURCH (Church of St Barbara)

Built in the 7th century, its lofty wooden roof probably dates to Fatimid times. The relics of St Barbara are in the right-hand sanctuary. She had the misfortune, so legend goes, to be born in the 3rd century to a pagan father, who, on discovering that she was a Christian, turned her over to the Roman authorities to be tortured and beheaded. (See page 37.)

Turn left out of the church to the gateway crowned with the Star of David.

6 BEN EZRA SYNAGOGUE

This is the oldest synagogue in Egypt, restored in the 12th century by the Rabbi of Jerusalem, Abraham Ben Ezra, though probably converted from a church in the 9th century. A far older tradition claims that Jeremiah came here to preach after Nebuchadnezzar had destroyed Jerusalem in the 6th century BC. (See page 32.)

redundant. The interior is intricately decorated with pointed arches, cedar panelling and translucent ivory screens. The carved marble pulpit is the finest in Egypt. On the right-hand wall is a 10th-century icon of the _Virgin and Child_, and next to it an icon of St Mark, by tradition the founder of Christianity in Egypt. (See page 35.)

Return to Sharia Mari Girgis, turn right, and follow the walls, passing the two Roman towers until you come to a small stairway which leads you to a passage through the walls. At the end of the street turn right.

4 ABU SARGA CHURCH (Church of St Sargius)

The Church of Abu Sarga, thought to date from the 5th century, is one of the oldest surviving churches in Egypt. According to tradition the Holy Family found refuge in the crypt below, once a cave, after their flight from Herod.

St. SARGIUS CHURCH
The Oldest Church in Egypt

WHERE THE HOLY FAMILY LIVED FOR SOME TIME DURING THEIR STAY IN EGYPT

Cairo Environs

*A*round 3100BC, Upper and Lower Egypt were united under the rule of Menes, who established the First Dynasty and founded Memphis as his capital. Built only for the duration of the living, the palaces, shrines and houses were made of mud brick. But at its necropolis of Saqqâra, the tombs of the dead were built of stone to endure eternity. Saqqâra was the world's first 'city' of stone. Some of its tombs, *mastabas,* resembled the single-storey houses of the living at Memphis, while the pharaoh Zoser had a grander idea. By placing a succession of ever smaller *mastabas* one on top of the other, he created his Step Pyramid. Subsequently, both to the north and south of Saqqâra, over 80 pyramids were constructed during the early Old Kingdom period, of which the Great Pyramids at Gîza are the largest and most famous.

GÎZA PYRAMIDS COMPLEX

The long straight road from Cairo passes through the built-up suburb of Gîza and finally curves sharply to the left and mounts the desert plateau. Before you is the Pyramid of Cheops, the oldest and largest of the three Gîza Pyramids. Beyond stand the pyramids of Chephren and Mycerinus, in descending order of age and size along a southwest axis, each identically oriented 8.5 degrees west of magnetic north. Built between 2600BC and 2525BC, they were probably aligned precisely with the North Star.

Near the edge of the desert and accessible by boat during the inundation was a modest valley chapel. From it led a walled-in causeway upwards to the funerary temple on the east side of the pyramid, where the soul of the dead pharaoh could emerge from its tomb to partake of the offered feasts. Not all of these structures have survived. On the sides of the Pyramid of Cheops wooden solar boats have been found in pits (see page 46) and there are smaller pyramids, some for royal wives, as well as rows of flat-topped tombs called *mastabas* for nobles and princes of the blood.

PYRAMID OF CHEOPS

Once all the pyramids had smooth sides of polished stone, but the casing on the Pyramid of Cheops has entirely gone and you see instead the underlying tiered courses of 2,500,000 limestone blocks. Inside, a descending corridor reaches a chamber in the bedrock left unfinished, possibly because of flooding, while a detour off the ascending corridor leads to the so-called Queen's Chamber.

Far grander is the ascending Great Gallery, which leads to the King's Chamber. On the north and south walls

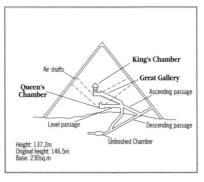

CHEOPS PYRAMID

King's Chamber
Air shafts
Great Gallery
Queen's Chamber
Ascending passage
Level passage
Descending passage
Unfinished Chamber

Height: 137.2m
Original height: 146.5m
Base: 230sq.m

GÎZA PYRAMIDS COMPLEX

At the western edge of Gîza, on the desert plateau above the Mena House Oberoi Hotel. 11km west of Cairo. Pyramids, Sphinx and Chephren's valley temple (admission charge) – open: daily 8am–4.30pm; Solar Boat Museum (additional charge) – open: daily 9am–4pm. For the Sound and Light performances, see page 47.

chambers, otherwise the King's Chamber contains neither inscriptions nor decorations, and its sarcophagus was found empty.

The great pyramid of Cheops

of this, a metre above the floor, you can see the ventilation shafts which reach to the surface of the pyramid. The weight of 95m of pyramid sits above your head, but the pressure is redirected away from the burial chamber by five successive relieving chambers above the granite roofing slabs. Cheops' name was found inscribed in the relieving

PYRAMID OF CHEPHREN

Chephren's Pyramid is almost as large as Cheops' and can seem larger because it stands on higher ground. The impression of greater height is also helped by the intact casing stones towards the top. Its interior, however, is less interesting. Its tomb chamber also contained an empty sarcophagus. Though all three Pyramids seemed sealed when entered during the 19th century, in fact they had each been looted at some ancient time.

PYRAMID OF MYCERINUS

At 66.5m in height, this is the smallest of the three main pyramids. A 9th-century caliph attempted to demolish the pyramids altogether, starting with that of Mycerinus. Eight months and 170,000 blocks of stone later, he gave up, leaving the gouge you see on its north face.

SOLAR BOAT MUSEUM

Some say that solar boats were built to ferry the pharaoh as he followed the sun god across the skies. Five solar boat pits have been found round the base of the Pyramid of Cheops. The first three were empty, but then in 1954, and again in 1987, two perfectly preserved, though dismantled, boats of Syrian cedar were discovered. The latter has been left within its pit, but the former, a graceful craft 4,600 years old and 43m long, has

PYRAMIDS OF GÎZA

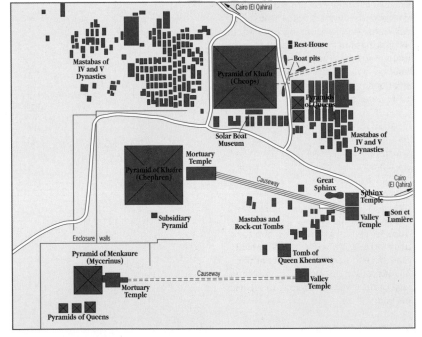

been reassembled and put on display in the specially-built museum at the south face of the Pyramid of Cheops.

SOUND AND LIGHT

The Sphinx plays the role of narrator in this booming and atmospheric programme telling the story of the Pyramids. Bring a sweater; even in summer the evenings can get cool.

THE SPHINX

A limestone outcrop was left standing in the quarry from which many of the blocks for Cheops' Pyramid were cut. His son Chephren had the idea of shaping it into a figure with a lion's body and a god's face – though perhaps the face is Chephren's own.

The Turks used the Sphinx for target practice in the 16th century and shot off its nose. The beard is at the British Museum. Though 20m high and 48.5m long, the Sphinx may not seem as large as you might imagine, as much of its bulk crouches within the quarry. The poor quality of its stone has contributed to its erosion.

VALLEY TEMPLE OF CHEPHREN

By the south flank of the Sphinx, Chephren's valley temple has been well preserved by its long burial under the sands. Majestically and simply assembled from pink Aswân granite, its square monolithic pillars support massive architraves. Some authorities think Chephren's mummification took place here; it is more generally agreed that this is where the 'Opening of the Mouth' ceremony took place, the *ka* or soul of the pharaoh entering and leaving his body.

Cheops' funerary solar boat

SOUND AND LIGHT

The Sound and Light pavilion faces the Sphinx and is signposted left off the main road to the Pyramids, 1km before the Mena House Oberoi Hotel, 10km west of Cairo's Midan el Tahrir. Tel: 3857928. There are two performances nightly, at 6.30 and 7.30pm (times differ according to season), in varying languages as follows: Monday – English and French; Tuesday – French and Italian; Wednesday – English and French; Thursday – Arabic and English; Friday – English and French; Saturday – English and Spanish. Sunday – French and German. Admission charge.

MEMPHIS

Most probably beginning as a fortress from which Menes controlled the land and water routes between Upper and Lower Egypt, Memphis was capital of the country throughout the Old Kingdom. Though New Kingdom Egypt was ruled from Thebes, Memphis remained a great metropolis until overtaken by Ptolemaic Alexandria. Today, however, centuries of Nile mud have swallowed Memphis entirely and there is little to see.

COLOSSUS OF RAMSES II

The New Kingdom pharaoh Ramses II was one of those who continued to embellish Memphis with great buildings and statues, including a pair of colossal statues of himself which probably stood outside the Temple of Ptah. Hauled out of the mud in 1820, one now stands outside the main Cairo railway station, and the other was offered to the British Museum – which failed to collect. And so here it lies, flat on its back, specially encased within a modern building. Other smaller statues stand or lie about in the surrounding gardens, including a large alabaster sphinx of the New Kingdom.

MUMMIFICATION BEDS

Across the road from the garden with its sphinx are the alabaster mummification beds where the bodies of the Apis bulls were soaked in a liquid containing natron (a natural salt) to dehydrate them in preparation for burial (see the **Serapeum**, page 51).

TEMPLE OF PTAH

The faint remains of this temple to the venerated god of Memphis lie water-logged near the mummification beds.

> **MEMPHIS**
> The ruins of Memphis are at the village of Mit Rahina, 3km from El Badrashein, on the west bank of the Nile, south of Cairo. Memphis is 32km south of Cairo by road, 21km south of the Gîza Pyramids, and 6km southeast from Saqqâra. It is included in most tours to Saqqâra; otherwise the only practical way of getting here is by taxi. Open: daily 9am–4pm. Admission charge.

Impressive statue of Ramses II

The 18th-century BC Alabaster Sphinx, surrounded by palm-lined pathways

SAQQÂRA

The sands wash about your feet nearly everywhere at Saqqâra, which has far more of a desert feel about it than Gîza. Named for Sokkar, the Memphite god of the dead, this was a necropolis for over 3,000 years, though most of its greatest monuments belong to the Old Kingdom. It was here that the ancient Egyptians first put into practice on a grand scale their attempt to defeat time – by replacing the perishable mud brick of their homes and shrines at Memphis with eternal replicas in stone.

MASTABA OF AKHTI-HOTEP AND PTAH-HOTEP

Belonging to the priest Ptah-Hotep and his father, the vizier Akhti-Hotep, this Fifth Dynasty double *mastaba* is outstanding for the variety and quality of its coloured reliefs.

The entrance corridor has reliefs in progress, the preliminary drawings in red with the master's corrections in black. Across a pillared hall you enter Ptah-Hotep's tomb chamber. A relief on the right wall shows Ptah-Hotep in the panther-skin of a high priest, seated at a cornucopian offering table, a goblet raised to his lips. A catalogue of daily events fills the left wall, including boys and girls playing games and a cow giving birth. The details are vivid: notice, for example, the hare emerging from its hole with a cricket in its mouth. Above the entrance you see Ptah-Hotep preparing for his day, a manicurist at his hands, a pedicurist at his feet, musicians entertaining him, with dogs and a pet monkey near by. Across the pillared hall is the similar, but less finely decorated, tomb chamber of Akhti-Hotep.

SAQQÂRA

Saqqâra is on the desert plateau above Memphis, 30km south of Cairo by road, 19km south of the Gîza Pyramids, and 6km northwest from Memphis. The only practical ways of getting here are by tour or taxi, or by horse or camel across the desert from the Gîza Pyramids (see page 52). Open: daily 9am–5pm. Admission charge.

Part of the extensive Sed Festival complex, at Zoser's Step Pyramid

MASTABA OF MERERUKA

Mereruka was vizier to a Sixth-Dynasty pharaoh and his 32-room *mastaba* is the largest at Saqqâra. The entry passage shows him painting a picture of the seasons and playing a board game to pass away eternity, while the first three chambers are decorated with scenes of hunting, furniture-making and goldsmiths at work. At the far end of the *mastaba*, in a chapel with six pillars, is a statue of Mereruka himself. The scenes to the left of this show the domestication of gazelles, goats and hyenas.

MASTABA OF TI

The reliefs in Ti's beautifully decorated funerary chamber rival those of Ptah-Hotep's, and exceed them in variety. The highlight here is a relief of Ti sailing through the marshes. The scene is full of symbolism, for this is Ti fighting against the forces of evil as represented by the

hunted hippopotamus, and of chaos represented by the fish and birds. The crocodile, at once being bitten by and biting the hippopotamus, was sacred and represents good.

Through a slot in the far wall, in what is called the *serdab*, you can see a statue of Ti. Here his soul or *ka* awaited the offerings brought to the chamber. Ti was overseer of royal farms and mortuary temples in the Fifth Dynasty. He was also the royal hairdresser. Looking into his *serdab*, you will notice that his hair, or wig, is well done.

PYRAMID OF UNAS

Unas was the last pharaoh of the Fifth Dynasty, and the 350 years from the Step Pyramid through the Great Pyramids at Gîza to this heap of rubble mark the rise and fall of the Old Kingdom sun cult. Though its core was shoddily built of loose stone and rubble,

Zoser's 'stairway to heaven'

the pyramid is safe and fascinating to enter, for the tomb chamber is entirely covered with inscriptions celebrating eternal life and the newly-popular resurrection cult of Osiris.

THE SERAPEUM

The Serapeum, where the Apis bulls were buried, is the strangest place at Saqqâra. Long, gloomily-lit, rock-cut galleries beneath the desert are lined with gigantic vaults, each vault containing a bull-sized black sarcophagus. For generation after generation, these Apis bulls were buried like kings, for they were believed to be incarnations of Ptah, the god of Memphis. The oldest galleries date back to the reign of Ramses II, though those open to the public belong to the time of the Ptolemies (see **Mummification Beds**, page 48).

STEP PYRAMID OF ZOSER

The Step Pyramid is the central piece of an extensive funerary complex built for the Third Dynasty pharaoh Zoser, who lived around 2700BC. Surrounded by an enclosure wall probably built in imitation of the city walls of Memphis, this first pyramid, 62m high, was created by placing a series of ever smaller *mastabas* one on top of the other.

The **Great South Court**, with its frieze of cobras, and the shrines in the Heb-Sed Court next to it, represent the ritual Heb-Sed race run in Memphis by the pharaoh during his 30th jubilee celebrations, impressing and reinvigorating a united Upper and Lower Egypt with his spiritual strength.

There is a relief of Zoser running the Heb-Sed race in the **South Tomb**, which is decorated with blue faïence tiles. It is reached via a deep shaft.

Passing along the east side of the Step Pyramid you come to the **House of the South**, its lotus capitals symbolising Upper Egypt, and the **House of the North**, with papyrus capitals on its graceful columns to symbolise Lower Egypt. Against the north side of the pyramid is the *serdab*, in which stands a *ka* statue of Zoser. His eyes are forever fixed on the North Star, the star which never sets and so never dies.

SAQQÂRA

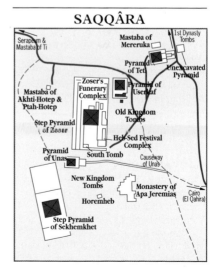

Gîza to Saqqâra

This journey across the desert and along the edge of the cultivation can be done by either horse or camel. It allows you to see several rarely visited pyramids and sun temples along the way. *Allow 3 hours in each direction, plus time to look around Saqqâra.* Alternatively, ride to Saqqâra and return to Gîza by taxi.

Start from the stables behind the Sound and Light pavilion, which is the best place to hire your mount.

1 GÎZA PYRAMIDS
You pass a modern Muslim cemetery on your left and head south across the sands, though you will always notice the cultivation of the Nile Valley to the east. The encroaching outskirts of Cairo soon disappear from sight and behind you there is a wonderful view of the Gîza Pyramids (see pages 44–7), which are Third Dynasty, standing alone on the desert plateau.
After about an hour and a quarter you come to two pyramids.

2 ZAWIYAT EL ARYAN PYRAMIDS
The northerly **Unfinished Pyramid**, abandoned during the Fourth Dynasty some time after the Gîza Pyramids, is surrounded by unused granite and limestone blocks. Fifteen minutes to the southeast, and nearer the cultivation, the **Layer Pyramid** is older than those at Gîza and belongs to the Third Dynasty. Built of small blocks it was perhaps meant to be a step pyramid.
About half an hour south, near the cultivation (where roses are the local speciality), are two sun temples.

3 ABU GHURAB SUN TEMPLES
The sun was always venerated by the ancient Egyptians. It is said that pyramids and obelisks, with a pyramid-shape at the top and sometimes covered with gold and silver, imitated the sun's

rays spreading across the earth. In the courtyard of the northerly Fifth Dynasty **Sun Temple of Nyuserre** stand an altar and the base of a solar obelisk. The obelisk has vanished, but you can climb up within the base for views across the desert.

Immediately to the southeast, passing by the Sun Temple of Userkaf, are the pyramids of Abusir.

4 ABUSIR PYRAMIDS

The northernmost **Pyramid of Sahure** is badly damaged, though you can crawl through a narrow passage into its tomb chamber and also climb to the summit. From here there is a fine panorama of the other Fifth-Dynasty pyramids in this cluster and their attendant mortuary temples. The group is named after the nearby village.

Continuing on, you pass the pyramids of **Nyuserre, Neferikare** and **Neferefre**. Neither the first nor last of these was ever finished owing to the early deaths of their pharaohs.

Neferikare also died early, but work continued, although what had begun with red granite and limestone was completed in mud brick.

5 APPROACHING SAQQÂRA

You can now clearly see the Step Pyramid and other structures at Saqqâra (see pages 49–51), no more than half an hour's ride south, and beyond that the **Red Pyramid** and the **Bent Pyramid** at Dahshur, both built by a Fourth-Dynasty pharaoh, together with another collapsed pyramid. Dahshur is normally off limits to tourists.

A camel will cost more to hire than a horse and is more exhilarating to ride, but be sure there is plenty of padding round the pommel. Most people, however, will find a horse more comfortable over this distance. Outside the summer months bring something warm to wear; the desert can get very windy and chilly.

Excursions From Cairo

THE DELTA

Whatever your interest in its ancient sites, there is fascination in a drive or train ride through the green and watery landscape of the Nile Delta, the river's last great outpouring before it reaches the Mediterranean coast. It is extraordinarily flat, and the sky is vast. The sails of feluccas billow amid fields furrowed by canals. Buffalo turn wheels for grinding or pumping, and brightly coloured figures move through an abundance of cotton, rice and maize.

In antiquity the Nile had seven arms here. Now it has only two, one flowing into the sea at Dumyât (Damietta), the other at Rashid (Rosetta). As arms dried up or changed course, cities were

abandoned, often disappearing beneath the mud. In Upper Egypt, where the river has been confined to its narrow valley, much of the past has been preserved. In the Delta, history has too often been erased.

Yet the Delta knew greatness. From their capital in the Eastern Delta the Hyksos, a foreign people of uncertain origin, ruled over the whole of Egypt during the Second Intermediate Period, and in the Eastern Delta, too, was the Land of Goshen mentioned in *Genesis* and *Exodus*. The dynasty of Seti I had its roots in the Delta, and his son, Ramses II, built his northern capital, Pi-Ramses, here. Throughout the first millennium BC the Delta dominated the affairs of Egypt, various dynasties having their capitals at Tanis, Bubastis and Sais. The Delta's importance became all the greater when the Ptolemies built their capital at Alexandria.

BUBASTIS

Near Zagazig, Bubastis is one of the most ancient sites in Egypt. The name means House of the Goddess Bastet, who was represented as a lioness, and later as a graceful domestic cat. Her much ruined temple, founded during the Old Kingdom but rebuilt during the Twenty-Second Dynasty, can be seen here. Beneath it are galleries for the burial of cats.

3km south of Zagazig, along the road to Bilbeis. Open: daily 9am–4pm. Free. Service taxis (which will drop you off at Bubastis), buses and trains all run the 80km from Cairo to Zagazig.

Winter visitor – the grey heron

DUMYÂT (Damietta)

Situated 15km from the Mediterranean on a narrow strip of land between the eastern arm of the Nile and Lake Manzala, Dumyât is a thriving port and industrial centre, preserving numerous mansions of the Ottoman period. Birdwatchers are attracted to the lake, in fact a brackish lagoon reaching eastwards towards Port Said, which is home to pelicans, storks, flamingos and egrets.

Famous at the time of the Crusades as Damietta, St Louis of France landed here in 1249 but was captured and ransomed. During an earlier attack on the city in 1218, St Francis of Assisi courageously crossed enemy lines and offered to enter a fiery furnace on the condition that should he come out alive, the sultan and his people would convert to Christianity. The sultan replied by giving the saint a lesson in humanity and common sense, saying that gambling with one's life was not a valid proof of one's God.

210km northeast of Cairo and served by train and bus.

VISITING

Like the arms of the Nile itself, the principal roads and railway lines fan out northwards from Cairo, while links between the Eastern and Western Delta are poor. The Western Delta can be visited *en route* to Alexandria, which is linked to Cairo by the main railway line and the Agricultural Road, while Rashid (Rosetta – see page 73) should be visited from Alexandria itself. Sites in the Eastern Delta are best visited by making a loop around Zagazig, while Dumyât would be a separate excursion.

Bedouin girl from Siwa Oasis

PI-RAMSES

Mentioned in *Exodus 1:11* and *12:37* as
the city built for the pharaoh by the
afflicted children of Israel, and as their
point of departure out of Egypt, under
Moses' leadership, the site of Pi-Ramses
is thought to be marked by the negligible
ruins found at Qantir.
*Qantir, near Faqus. 45km northeast of
Zagazig.*

SAIS

Though at times capital during the Late
Period, there is nothing to see today at
Sais. The site has suffered from the
activities of the *sebakhin,* an interesting
example of how Egypt lives upon its
past. In a land where wood is a rarity
and animal dung has been used for fuel,
the *fellahin* have turned to the debris
mounds or *koms* of ancient towns. These
yield a rich soil called *sebakh* which is
used as a fertiliser. The once royal city
of Sais is now a waterlogged hole in the
ground.
30km to the northwest of Tanta.

TANIS

Egyptologists once argued that Tanis
was the site of Pi-Ramses, but despite its
fall from Biblical grace it nevertheless
possesses the most impressive ruins in
the Delta. It has even been called the
'Thebes of the North'.

The **Temple of Amun** is spectacular
for its fallen colossal statuary, and you
can enter the royal tombs of its Twenty-
First- and Twenty-Second-Dynasty
pharaohs, whose capital this was. The
splendid gold masks, inlaid jewellery and
silver sarcophagus discovered here in
1939, and rivalling the treasures of
Tutankhamun, are now in the Egyptian

Antiquities Museum in Cairo (see page 33).

A sacred lake and the remains of two other temples are evident within the enclosure walls.

Near San el Hagar. 74km northeast of Zagazig. Some tours come here, otherwise you must take a taxi and have it wait for you. Open: daily 9am–4pm. Admission charge.

TANTA

This non-descript city, with a population of 250,000, is Egypt's fifth largest. It jumps to life at the end of the October cotton harvest, when as many as two million people, from the Delta and all round the Arab world, attend the joyous *moulid* centred round the mosque and tomb of a 13th-century *sufi*, Said Ahmed el Badawi.

90km northwest of Cairo, on the railway line to Alexandria.

ZAGAZIG

Dating only from the 1820s, this is the birthplace of Ahmed Orabi, leader of the 1882 revolt against British influence. Zagazig is a good place to begin a tour

Typical Delta architecture – note the brickwork and decoration

of the Eastern Delta. Its **Orabi Museum** contains objects from nearby Bubastis.

85km northeast of Cairo from where it is well-served by service-taxi, bus and train. Orabi Museum open: 9am–1pm. Closed: Tuesday.

THE TANTA *MOULID*

Reminders of Egypt's past are found not only in its stones. The *moulid* at Tanta is not linked, like so many other Muslim festivals, to the lunar calendar but is fixed to coincide with the autumn harvest, traditionally a time of joy. During the festival large quantities of sugar-coated nuts called *hubb el Azziz* ('seeds of the Beloved Prophet') are consumed – a favourite Egyptian delicacy since ancient times.

A burlesque side-show to the more serious ritual of the *moulid,* known

locally as *zeffa el Sharamit,* the procession of the prostitutes, recalls the licentious celebrations at Bubastis described by the 5th-century BC Greek historian, Herodotus. Barges full of clapping and singing men and women would draw close to riverbank towns so that the women could 'shout abuse at the women of the place or start dancing, or stand up and hitch up their skirts'. As many as 700,000 people came to Bubastis then, and 'more wine is consumed than during all the rest of the year.'

The Faiyûm and the Western Desert

THE FAIYÛM

Though almost entirely surrounded by the Western Desert, the Faiyûm is not a true oasis because it depends on the Nile. Failure to maintain the Faiyûm's irrigation system during the late Roman period caused Lake Qarun to shrink, leaving ghost towns all round its desert perimeter (see pages 60–1).

Revival began under the British, and the Faiyûm now possesses 2,300km of capillary canals – equivalent to the entire length of the Nile through Egypt. Cereals, vegetables, fruits and flowers grow again in wonderful profusion, and increasing numbers of visitors are attracted to the Faiyûm as much for its rural charm as for its ancient sites.

Donkey-powered water wheel

KOM AUSHIM (Ancient Karanis)

Offering a good panorama of the lake and oasis from the rim of the Faiyûm depression, Karanis is the most accessible of the abandoned Ptolemaic towns. Beyond the roadside museum are ancient streets and houses, and two temples dedicated to crocodile gods.

Served by buses and service taxis plying the desert road between Cairo (76km) and Medinet el Faiyûm (30km). Museum open: 9am–4pm. Closed: Monday. Admission charge.

MEDINET EL FAIYÛM

All roads and canals radiate from this unattractive market centre, site of the Ptolemaic city of Crocodilopolis.

Obelisk of Sesostris I

This 12th-Dynasty obelisk stands at a roundabout as you arrive from Cairo.

Qaytbay Mosque

This Mameluke mosque, which has columns from ancient Crocodilopolis, is a 10-minute walk west from the tourist office at the town centre.

Souk

Near the Qaytbay Mosque is a warren of market streets, some covered, selling food, spices, copperware and jewellery.

Waterwheels

Four waterwheels groan away outside the Cafeteria el Medina by the tourist office at the centre of town. There are 200 throughout the oasis. In 30 minutes you can walk to the Seven Waterwheels, a Faiyûm landmark, north of town.

> **THE FAIYÛM**
> 100km southwest of Cairo. The Faiyûm is reached by bus or service taxi to Medinet el Faiyûm.

OASES OF THE WESTERN DESERT

BAHARÎYA
White-walled houses and a 6th-century Coptic church mark the old quarter of **Bawiti** on a ridge, Qarat el-Farargi, overlooking palm groves. One kilometre west is the sister village of **El Qasr**, its houses incorporating stones from a 26th-Dynasty temple and a Roman arch.

DAKHLA
Dakhla is the most beautiful of the oases. Its two main towns are **Mut**, with hot springs near by at Mut Talata, and, 27km to the west, **El Qasr**, the original fortified settlement of the oasis with a Mameluke mosque and a Roman temple close by.

FARAFRA
Isolated Farafra has a picturesque old quarter and walled palm groves for delightful walks. The atmosphere is religiously conservative.

EL KHÂRGA
El Khârga town is a developed and unromantic place, though at ancient **Hibis**, on its northern outskirts, there is a temple of Amun, and 1km beyond at **Baqawat**, there is an early Christian necropolis.

SIWA
The well-preserved temple of Ammon rises from vast groves of date palms and fruit trees. Here Alexander came to consult the oracle and was told he was a god. Siwa continues to deliver romance, and though its crumbling fortified village has been abandoned for newer houses, tradition remains strong.

Veiled and berobed women drape themselves in silver jewellery, Berber is spoken instead of Arabic, and local festivals and marriage customs are still observed – though homosexual marriage was discontinued earlier this century.

OASES OF THE WESTERN DESERT
With the exception of Siwa near the Libyan border, which is reached by travelling west from Alexandria to Mersa Matruh and then south, the oases of the Western Desert are linked by a 1,000km road looping out from Cairo and back to the Nile at Asyût. All can be reached by bus and service taxi; and there are flights to Kharga.

The Faiyûm

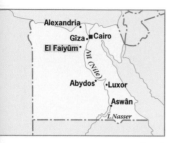

When in late Roman times the irrigation system of the Faiyûm began to fail through neglect, a number of Ptolemaic towns and more ancient sites around the periphery of the oasis were abandoned to the advancing sands. Medinet el Faiyûm is the transport hub from which to start each visit. The tourist office at the centre of town, by the café with the four waterwheels, can give you information on the cost and location of private taxis, service taxis, bijous (covered pick-up trucks running on fixed routes for a fixed fare) and buses. *Allow 1 day if you have a car. By public transport, select one or two sights to visit.*

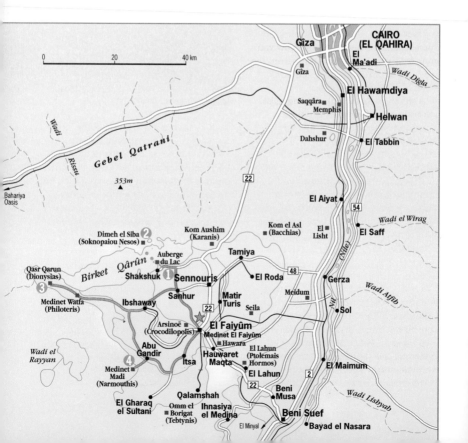

The direct route to Lake Qarun is via Sanhur. From here, you can approach the Auberge du Lac from the east or by way of the lakeside village of Shakshuk.

1 AUBERGE DU LAC

The Auberge du Lac was originally King Farouk's hunting lodge but is now a hotel. From its veranda you can look out over the lake, which attracts great numbers of migratory birds, including the pink flamingo, and, in winter, thousands of ducks.

From here or Shakshuk you can hire a boatman for an hour's journey across the lake to Dimeh el Siba.

2 DIMEH EL SIBA

In Ptolemaic times this was a lakeside town called *Soknopaiou Nesos*. Now you must walk up a steep 3km track from the north shore of the lake to reach this scene of majestic desolation.

A 400m processional way begins at what was the lakeshore and passes through the town gate to the **Temple of Soknopaios and Isis** with several reliefs, one of Ptolemy II praying before Amun. The settlement was a fortified caravan station, the launching point for the long journey across the desert to more distant oases.

There are service taxis from the Auberge du Lac, Shakshuk, and Medinet el Faiyûm to Ibshaway, then on to the village of Qasr Qarun near the western extremity of the lake.

3 QASR QARUN

Beside the village are the remains of the Ptolemaic settlement of **Dionysias,** its most notable feature a sandstone Ptolemaic temple dedicated to the crocodile god Sobek. You can explore its labyrinthine interior and climb up to

Remains of a mud-brick town

the roof for distant views over the oasis and desert.

To reach ancient Narmouthis, known as Medinet Madi, take a bus to Menshat Sef, a village south of Abu Gandir. Walking west from here, follow the canal, cross over the first bridge, and take the narrow track south. Within an hour you will see a stone hut on the desert's rise. Just beyond it is Medinet Madi.

4 MEDINET MADI

A processional way lined by lions and sphinxes approaches the Twelfth-Dynasty temple dedicated to Sobek and covered with numerous reliefs. The mud-brick remains of the town lie about, while an embankment to the north of the temple was in fact the storm beach of Lake Qarun.

Wadi Natrûn

*T*he Coptic monasteries of the Wadi Natrûn, once isolated in the Western Desert, now lie within sight of the 200km Desert Road built between Cairo and Alexandria in the 1930s. Founded early in the 4th century, they are among the oldest monasteries in the world. They look like fortresses, their great walls surrounding a central keep built in defence against Bedouin raids. Often rebuilt both within and without, nothing stands from before the 7th century. Today, these and other desert monasteries are at the heart of the spiritual revival of the Coptic Church, and their monks are recruited from the universities and the professions.

MONASTERY OF ST BARAMOUS
(Deir el Baramous)
Parts of the monastery Church of el Adra (the Virgin) date from the 9th century, and alongside it is the old refectory. From the 11m-high walls you can look down into its arbour-shaded courtyard and out into the surrounding desert where there are several hermits' caves.

MONASTERY OF ST BISHOI
(Deir Anba Bishoi)
From his tomb in the 9th-century Church of St Bishoi, the saint himself is said occasionally to reach out and shake the hands of believers. The atmosphere suggested by the tale, however, has been stripped away by much rebuilding and modernisation, making this the least interesting of the four monasteries.

MONASTERY OF ST MACARIUS
(Deir Abu Maqar)
You might almost think this a holiday village for monks when you enter the monastery courtyard surrounded by new cells, a refectory, library, guesthouse, bakery and other amenities. Nevertheless, much of ancient interest survives.

In the voluminous Church of St Macarius, the central domed sanctuary of John the Baptist, decorated with a winged cherub and the four creatures of the Apocalypse, is 7th-century. On the arch before the sanctuary are finely painted 11th-century scenes of Christ's burial. The three-storey keep, entered by a drawbridge, is also 11th-century. There are four churches within it, with wonderful paintings of saints and hermits on their walls.

Coptic monks, Monastery of the Syrians

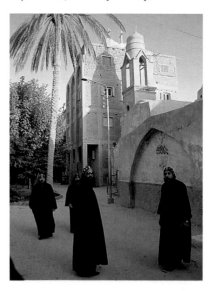

Fresco of the *Annunciation* in the Church of el Adra, Monastery of the Syrians

MONASTERY OF THE SYRIANS
(Deir el Suriani)

With a huge hull supporting a super-structure of domes, towers and crosses, this most fascinating of the four monasteries is like a great ship riding the waves of desert sand.

Its 10th-century Church of el Adra (the Virgin) is remarkable for the carved and inlaid wooden doors across the sanctuary, and more so for the beautiful frescos in the semidomes of the choir. On the right are the *Annunciation* and *Nativity*, on the left the *Dormition of the Virgin*. At the opposite end of the church is a grotto, said to have been the hermit's cell of St Bishoi long before the church was built.

From the Rest House, 95km north-west of Cairo on the west side of the Desert Road to Alexandria, a road runs 3km to Bir Hooker village. There the road forks, right 12km for the Monastery of Baramous, left 7km for the monasteries of the Syrians and St Bishoi, 500m from one another.

The Monastery of St Macarius is 15km further south. It is most easily reached from the Desert Road: 82km north of Cairo (13km before the Rest House), a road runs west for 8km to the monastery.

Buses and service taxis running between Cairo and Alexandria stop at the Rest House, where you can hire a local taxi. Alternatively, hire a taxi from Cairo for the day.

All four monasteries are generally open daily to both men and women from 10am to 5pm, but some or all may be closed in whole or in part during periods of fasting. See page 179 for details on visiting and staying overnight at Coptic monasteries.

CHRISTIANITY

Until the Arab invasion in AD641, Egypt was a Christian country, but within 500 years the majority of Egyptians had become Muslims. About 10 per cent of the population, however, has remained Christian and these are called Copts, a corruption of the Greek word for Egypt, *Aigyptos*.

As 90 per cent of Muslim Egyptians were also once Copts, it is impossible to distinguish physically between Copts and Muslims. Nor do they differ in language or culture. Both groups are proud to call themselves Egyptians.

St Mark is the legendary 1st-century founder of Christianity in Egypt. From its earliest roots among the Jews and Greeks of Alexandria, Christianity soon spread among the native population, where it resonated with – and indeed in some measure borrowed from – such ancient Egyptian notions as resurrection and the afterlife. Isis and the infant Horus, for example, resemble the Virgin and Child, and it was no accident that a native-born Egyptian theologian of Alexandria first pronounced Mary to be the Mother of God. Monasticism also began in Egypt and went on to make a profound spiritual impact on the wider world.

By the 5th century, the Roman and Byzantine Empires had split, and Egypt was ruled from Constantinople. Soon a theological argument, abetted by nationalist undercurrents, developed. In Constantinople and Rome, it was held

Above and left: Christian cemetery and church in Babylon, Old Cairo

Right: Relief carving with Christian motif, Museum of Antiquities, Luxor

that Christ had two separate natures, the human and the divine. Alexandrian theologians, while admitting the two natures, emphasised their unity. For this they were called monophysites (believers in only one nature), and were charged with heresy at the Ecumenical Council of Chalcedon in 451.

Had national pride not got in the way, the theological differences might have been overcome. But at the moment of the Arab invasion, Egypt was in a state of mutiny against the Byzantine Empire whose forces could do nothing but abandon the country. Over the centuries the Coptic Church turned in upon itself, preserving ancient rituals while failing to develop.

Nowadays, however, it is experiencing a renaissance and maintaining a flourishing congregation, while, in a new ecumenical spirit, links are being forged with Christian churches worldwide.

Alexandria

*A*lexandria is Egypt's major port and the country's second largest city, with a population of four million. Unlike the rest of the country, it is cool and wet in winter, with refreshing Mediterranean breezes during the heat of summer. Alexander the Great founded the city in 332BC on the site of a small fishing village, *Rhakotis*. He then built a causeway connecting the island of Pharos (where Ras el Tin Palace and Qaytbay Fort stand) to the mainland, creating two great harbours which became the basis of Alexandria's prosperity.

This spirit of invention was continued under Alexander's Greek successors, the Ptolemies, who built the famous Pharos lighthouse, established the Great Library, and founded the Mouseion, a research institute where remarkable advances were made in mathematics, engineering and medicine. Later still, Alexandria played a formative role in the development of Christian thought, adding the dimension of Greek philosophy to Jewish and Egyptian beliefs.

Little of this ancient and illustrious city survives, however. After the 7th-century Arab invasion, Alexandria declined. Refounded early in the 19th century by Mohammed Ali, foreigners were attracted by the promise of trading opportunities, especially in cotton. Cosmopolitan and lively, the city enjoyed a gilded age through to the 1950s, its hothouse atmosphere captured vividly in Lawrence Durrell's *Alexandria Quartet*.

Now somewhat provincial and down-at-heel, the city possesses little glamour and few ancient sites, but Alexandria's situation is charming and its past still haunts the fading streets.

ALEXANDRIA

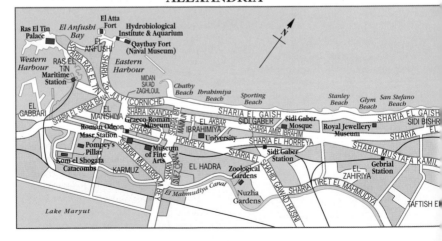

One of the great cities of antiquity, Alexandria is Egypt's largest port

ABU EL ABBAS AND BOUSEIRI MOSQUES

The domes and minarets of these adjacent mosques lend a graceful touch to the skyline of the Eastern Harbour (see page 71). The larger of the two is the Abu el Abbas Mosque, built in 1943 over a 13th-century tomb. Around it clusters the picturesque old quarter. Between it and the Corniche is the Bouseiri Mosque, twinkling with lights at night.

Overlooking the Corniche towards Qaytbay Fort. 2km northwest of Midan Sa'ad Zaghloul. Open: dawn until late. Free.

ANFUSHI TOMBS

Cut into the limestone ridge that formed the island of Pharos, these four tombs are basically Greek with Egyptian elements (see page 71). The walls are painted to give the impression of marble and tile. In the tomb furthest to the right there are scenes of a felucca and a warship of the type Cleopatra might have used to sail in to Actium.

At the western end of Sharia Ras el Tin. 2.5km northwest of Midan Sa'ad Zaghloul. Open: daily 9am–4pm. Closed: Friday 11.30am–1.30pm. Admission charge.

ATTARINE

There is everything from old postcards to antique furniture to fascinate you in this flea market area of Alexandria, which centres on Sharia el Attarine.

Sharia el Attarine runs south from Sharia Sidi el Mitwalli. 1km south of Midan Sa'ad Zaghloul. Shops open until 9pm.

COPTIC ORTHODOX CATHEDRAL OF ST MARK

The interior of the church is handsome. Note the plaque listing all the Coptic patriarchs, going right back to St Mark, the traditional founder of Christianity in Egypt.

Rue de l'Eglise Copte, west along Sharia Sa'ad Zaghloul from Sharia el Nebi Danyal. 400m southwest from Midan Sa'ad Zaghloul. Open: early morning until late. Free.

GRAECO-ROMAN MUSEUM

Filling the historical gap between the Egyptian Antiquities Museum and the Coptic Museum, both in Cairo, the Graeco-Roman Museum covers the fascinating period when Western culture overlaid and sometimes incorporated the native Egyptian world. Its spacious and uncluttered rooms are arranged around a central garden, making it a pleasant place to linger. Many of the exhibits are from Alexandria and its vicinity; the rest are from other areas of Greek settlement – the Delta, the Faiyûm and Middle Egypt.

Note the statue of Serapis in Room 6. This jolly looking god was invented by the Ptolemies, who combined the human look of Dionysios with the cult of the Apis bull in an effort to unite Greek and Egyptian culture. A giant statue of the Apis bull, found near Pompey's Pillar, stands in the centre of the same room. In Room 12 are sculpted heads of Alexander and Cleopatra.

The finest objects in the museum are the small Tanagra terracotta figures in Room 18A. They come from late 4th-century to early 2nd-century BC Alexandrian tombs of children, adolescents and young women. Prompted by the sadness of death in youth, they are delicately expressive of life's moment.

Sharia Mathaf, north off Sharia Horreya. 1km east of Midan Sa'ad Zaghloul. Open: daily 9am–4pm. Closed: Friday 11.30am–1.30pm. Admission charge.

KOM EL DIKKA

This area of excavation near the centre of Alexandria has revealed a Roman odeon (a theatre for musical performances), and a large complex of 3rd-century AD Roman baths. Streets and shops of the Ptolemaic period are gradually being unearthed, and columns and arches raised. The site gives you an idea of how much of the ancient city could be recovered – if only the modern city were knocked down.

Entrance on the south side of the large square, Midan el Gumhuriya, in front of the railway station. 1km southeast of Midan Sa'ad Zaghloul. Open: daily 9am–4pm. Closed: Friday 11.30am–1.30pm. Admission charge.

Mummy with Christian cross

Once used for music, the marble-terraced Roman theatre has seating for 700 to 800 people

KOM EL SHOGAFA CATACOMBS

The largest and weirdest tombs in Alexandria (see page 71).
West off Sharia Amud el Sawari. 2.5km south of Midan Sa'ad Zaghloul. Open: daily 9am–4pm. Closed: Friday 11.30am–1.30pm. Admission charge.

Nearby ———————————————
Pompey's Pillar.

MONTAZAH PALACE AND GARDENS

Built in Turko-Florentine style at the turn of the century by the Khedive Abbas II, this was the summer residence of the royal family. The palace is closed to the public, but from the outside, notice that the letter F is used as a recurring motif. A fortune teller had told King Fuad that the letter F would bring his family luck, whereupon he and his son Farouk gave all their children names beginning with F. Then, in 1951, Farouk married Narriman and neglected to change her name, and in January 1952 she bore him a son, Ahmed Fuad, the F relegated to second place. Six months later Farouk was out of a job.
16km northeast of Midan Sa'ad Zaghloul. Gardens open: 24 hours daily. Admission charge.

POMPEY'S PILLAR

See page 71.
Sharia Amud el Sawari. 2km south of Midan Sa'ad Zaghloul. Open: daily 9am–4pm. Closed: Friday 11.30am–1.30pm. Admission charge.

Nearby ———————————————
Kom el Shogafa Catacombs.

QAYTBAY FORT

The fort stands on the site of the famous Ptolemaic lighthouse (see page 71).
At the tip of the western arm of the Eastern Harbour. 3.5km northwest of Midan Sa'ad Zaghloul. Open: 9am–2pm. Closed: Friday 11.30am–1.30pm. Admission charge.

RAS EL TIN PALACE

See page 71.
At the eastern tip of the Western Harbour. 3km west of Midan Sa'ad Zaghloul. Closed to the public.

ROYAL JEWELLERY MUSEUM

Housed in the palace of an Egyptian princess, this collection covers the 150-year period from the rise of Mohammed Ali to the fall of King Farouk.
27 Sharia Ahmed Yehia, Glym. Open: daily 9am–4pm. Closed: Friday 11.30am–1.30pm. Admission charge.

Alexandria

Carriages, which can comfortably take two people, are the most delightful way to travel around Alexandria. Tell the driver where you wish to go. *Allow at least 3 hours.*

Begin outside the Cecil Hotel on the Corniche at Midan Sa'ad Zaghloul.

1 THE CECIL HOTEL
This Moorish pile, built in 1929, is something of a landmark. Somerset Maugham, Noel Coward and Lawrence Durrell have all signed its visitors' book. Take time to refresh yourself in its art deco tea lounge. Outside once stood the **Caesareum**,

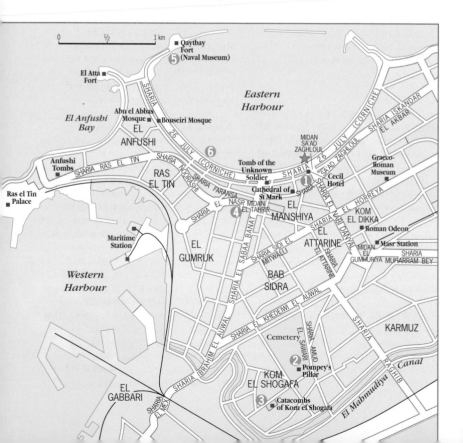

which Cleopatra built for Antony. There perhaps she committed suicide, and from there came Cleopatra's Needle, now in London, and the obelisk in New York's Central Park.

Head southwest to where Pompey's Pillar and Kom el Shogafa are close together.

2 POMPEY'S PILLAR

Wrongly attributed by the Crusaders to the 1st-century BC Roman general Pompey, the pillar was raised at the end of the 3rd century AD to the Emperor Diocletian. At its base are two pink granite sphinxes of the Ptolemaic period. This was once the acropolis of the city, and here also stood the Temple of Serapis, a Graeco-Egyptian god invented by the Ptolemies, which was destroyed by a Christian mob in AD391.

A short ride south is Kom el Shogafa.

3 KOM EL SHOGAFA CATACOMBS

This largest Roman funerary complex in Egypt dates from the 2nd century AD. A winding staircase leads to an underground rotunda encircled by sarcophagi. Next to it is the banqueting hall where relatives of the deceased saw him out with a feast. At the level below is the central tomb chamber, decorated in a weird blend of classical and Egyptian styles. Inside stand dog-headed Anubis and crocodile-headed Sobek, both dressed as Roman centurions. (See page 69.)

Head north to Midan el Tahrir.

4 MIDAN EL TAHRIR TO FORT QAYTBAY

In the square is an equestrian statue of Mohammed Ali who brought Alexandria back to life in the 19th century. From here, in Alexander's time, a causeway

Stanley Bay, along Alexandria's corniche

was built to the island of Pharos. Long ago silted up, its line is followed by Sharia Faransa which runs from the northwest corner of Midan el Tahrir through the picturesque old Egyptian quarter.

Towards the Western Harbour are the **Anfushi tombs** (see page 67), while on the headland overlooking the harbour is **Ras el Tin Palace** (see page 69). Here, on 26 July 1952, King Farouk abdicated and sailed into exile.

5 QAYTBAY FORT

The present 15th-century fort was built by Sultan Qaytbay on the site of, and partly from fragments of, the six-times taller Pharos lighthouse, which had been destroyed in a series of earthquakes. Dating from the reign of Ptolemy II Philadelphos and renowned as one of the seven wonders of the ancient world, the Pharos could, by means of a mirror, direct a beam of reflected sunlight or the light of a fire far out to sea. (See page 69.)

6 ALONG THE CORNICHE

Follow the graceful sweep of the Eastern Harbour back towards the Cecil Hotel, passing on your right the pleasing ensemble of the modern mosques of **Bouseiri** and, behind it, **Abu el Abbas**. (See page 67.)

Excursions from Alexandria

ABUSIR

The name Abusir contains, in transmuted form, the memory of a small ancient city, *Taposiris*. Though interesting and simple to get to, nobody comes, and few people know of its existence.

Taposiris stood at the western end of the same limestone ridge upon which Alexandria was built. Its ruins are slight, except for its tower and its temple. The enclosure walls of its **Temple of Osiris** are impressive and there are pylons to climb for fine views over the delicate green marshes of Lake Maryut to the south. To the north the sea is astonishingly turquoise against the burning white coastal sand. The innards of the temple are gone except for the foundations of an early church.

A few hundred metres to the east stands the tower, in fact a Roman lighthouse, built on the pattern but one-tenth the size of the Pharos.

Along the Mediterranean coast road. 45km west of Alexandria, unprotected, always open and free. A hired car or taxi is needed to get here.

EL ALAMEIN

The scene of the famous series of World War II battles is now marked by a museum with tanks and pieces of heavy artillery, while immediately to the east of the village is the starkly beautiful British Cemetery. The Italian and German cemeteries are respectively 8km and 12km further west.

On 17 July 1942, British General Auchinleck stopped Rommel's advance on Alexandria. Over the period 23 October to 5 November 1942, British Field Marshal Montgomery decisively defeated the Germans and put Rommel on the run. Within little more than six months the Germans and Italians were cleared from Africa altogether.

On the Mediterranean coast road. 106km west of Alexandria. Museum open: daily 9am–6pm, but closes at 3pm during Ramadan. Admission charge. Buses stop here between Alexandria and Mersa Matruh, but, though you can reserve a seat from Alexandria, you cannot at El Alamein, and will probably have to stand during the return journey. A hired car or taxi would be more practical.

The British War Cemetery, El Alamein

MERSA MATRUH

While *en route* to the oasis of Siwa, you might wish to pause here for the magnificent beaches outside this one-time fishing port, now something of a boom town.

On the coast. 290km west of Alexandria. Service taxis and fast non-stop buses make the journey in 4 hours, while buses stopping at El Alamein and Sîdi Abd el Rahman take 5 hours.

RASHID (Rosetta)

Founded in the 9th century AD, Rosetta flourished as Alexandria declined. During the 17th and 18th centuries, it was Egypt's most important port. Many of its houses of this period have recently been restored and constitute the finest examples in Egypt of Islamic domestic architecture outside Cairo. With the 19th-century refounding of Alexandria, Rosetta has in turn declined and is now a small agricultural market and fishing town, pleasantly situated on the western arm of the Nile, 10km from the sea.

The town is most famously associated with the discovery here by one of Napoleon's soldiers of the **Rosetta Stone**, now in the British Museum. Because its inscription in ancient hieroglyphics is repeated in Greek, in 1821 Jean François Champollion succeeded in deciphering the ancient Egyptian language, thereby opening up Egypt's pharaonic past.

67km east of Alexandria. Both buses and service taxis make the trip.

SÎDI ABD EL RAHMAN

This is an isolated upmarket resort with a beautiful white beach. Accommodation is almost impossible to book during summer, but you might like to stop here for a swim when visiting El Alamein.

On the Mediterranean coast. 26km west of El Alamein, 132km west of Alexandria. Though buses and service taxis stop here, it is likely to be standing room only on the bus back to Alexandria.

The museum at El Alamein displays tanks, weaponry and heavy artillery dating from World War II

East of the Nile

*T*o travel east of the Nile is to enter another world. The level, green and placid landscapes of Egypt's river and its Delta are left behind. Instead mountains line the Red Sea coast, while central and southern Sinai are harsh and rocky, as though in a state of geological eruption. There is also the remarkable sight of the Suez Canal, the ceaseless passage of ships like patrols along a border.

The impression of arriving at a frontier is due to a great rip in the Earth's surface which extends from Africa's Rift Valley in the south to the valley of the River Jordan in the north. The **Red Sea** is extremely deep and its coastal mountains rise over 2,000m. Along with its northern finger, the **Gulf of Aqaba**, its enclosed waters are exceptionally warm and settled, encouraging the formation of reefs and attracting the many brilliantly-coloured fish that make this one of the finest places in the world for scuba divers.

Sinai, too, offers adventure, not only along its coasts but for off-road enthusiasts wishing to explore its vast sandscapes in the north and the wild mountains and *wadis* of its central and southern interior. Tradition claims that Moses wandered among the jagged peaks in the south, an area of enormous historic significance, which accounts for the presence here of one of the most magnificent of all monasteries, St Catherine's.

EL ARÎSH

Until recently, El Arîsh was merely a Bedouin settlement on the Mediterranean coast of Sinai. Now it is the largest town on the peninsula and is being developed as a tourist resort, with new luxury hotels along its magnificent palm-fringed beach.

On Sinai's northern coast road. 278km northeast of Cairo via Ismailia and the Suez Canal ferry-crossing at Qantara. Alternatively, you can travel via the tunnel north of Suez, in which case the Cairo-El Arîsh distance totals 437km. There are also flights from Cairo.

DAHAB

On the east coast of Sinai, and beautifully set against a backdrop of mountains, Dahab has two lifestyles; that of the fastidious tourist town to the south, and the ghetto-blasting, beach-bum scene 3km north on the edge of the pre-existing Bedouin village. But the great attraction is the reef fish. The tourist town offers the best diving shops and the best reefs.

494km from Cairo via the Suez tunnel. The bus takes 8 hours. There are flights from Cairo to Sharm el Sheikh.

FEIRAN OASIS

The Feiran Oasis, the largest in Sinai, is like a secret garden of palms, tamarisks and wheat set between towering mountain walls. Monks and hermits lived in the oasis during the early Christian centuries. Amid a plantation here, an avenue of column drums and capitals salvaged from ancient buildings leads up to a 19th-century chapel dedicated to Moses. Behind it are the ruins of a 4th-century bishop's palace.

South-central Sinai. 250km from the Suez tunnel en route to St Catherine's Monastery, and 395km east of Cairo (5½ hours by bus).

HURGHADA

Once a fishing village, Hurghada has become the centre for Egypt's Red Sea oil operations. Near the town the sea is too polluted with oil and sewage for swimming. Instead you should check into one of the resort hotels a few kilometres to the south, with their clean private beaches. The town has a new aquarium, but you should really hire a boat to the reefs and islands, where you can submerge yourself in the crystalline

For off-road destinations in Sinai and the Red Sea mountains, see pages 130–1; for more on the Red Sea resorts, see page 140.

waters to enjoy a brilliantly coloured submarine world.

On the Red Sea coast road. 406km south of Suez, 550km southeast of Cairo (7 hours by bus), and 235km northeast of Luxor. Flights from Cairo and Luxor. An aquarium is on Sharia el Bahr. Open: daily 9am–10pm. Admission charge.

Bedouins in the Sinai

ISMAILIA

Midway along the Suez Canal, Ismailia is its operational headquarters. The town owes its character to the British, and its waterside district of wide, clean streets with suburban-style houses in well-planted gardens looks remarkably like a tropical England.

Among these streets is the town museum, its exhibits recalling ancient attempts to dig the canal. That job was finally accomplished in the 1860s under the direction of Ferdinand de Lesseps, whose house on the main street as you come in from Cairo is also now a museum. On the canal is a swimming club with sandy beach, deck chairs and refreshments, and hypnotic views of supertankers parading by.

120km northeast of Cairo, served by trains, buses and service taxis. Town museum open: daily 9am–4pm. Closed: Friday 11am–2pm. Admission charge. De Lesseps' House open: daily 9am–4pm. Closed: Tuesday. Admission charge.

NUWEIBA

Less attractively situated than Dahab, Nuweiba is also somewhat down-at-heel and quiet, and there are few diving facilities for exploring its fine reefs.

On the Gulf of Aqaba, on the eastern coast of Sinai. The distance from Cairo via the Suez tunnel is 560km. The bus takes 8½ hours. There are flights from Cairo to Sharm el Sheikh.

PORT SAID

At the north end of the Suez Canal and with town beaches along the Mediterranean, Port Said prospers owing to its duty-free status. Visitors arriving from inland must show their passports. Along Sharia el Gumhuriya, two streets back from the canal, there

Sharia el Gumhuriya, Port Said

are many beautiful old wooden buildings with balconies dating from the last century and reminiscent of the French Quarter in New Orleans. Its famous landmark, familiar especially to sea travellers, is the Suez Canal Building overlooking the canal itself, its gleaming white colonnade crowned with three brilliant green domes. One way of getting a good view of the canal is to take the commuter ferry over to Port Fuad, a voyage from Africa to Asia.

Northeast of Cairo, from which trains and buses cover the 200km via Ismailia in 4 hours.

ST ANTONY'S MONASTERY
(Deir Anba Antunius)

Surrounded by 2km of walls standing 12m high, St Antony's Monastery is dramatically set against the cliffs of the Eastern Desert plateau. St Antony, who died in 356, is the world's first historically documented Christian hermit and the inspiration for the monastic movement. This monastery, founded by his disciples, claims to be the earliest in the world. It was said to have once rivalled the Greek Orthodox Monastery of St Catherine in beauty, but it was sacked by Bedouins in the 15th century. Walk along the parapets of the 10th-century walls, climb the 16th-century four-storey keep, and look at the numerous frescos of prophets and saints inside the church which date from the 12th century. Against the south wall is the Spring of St Antony, while a 2km path climbs up behind the monastery to St Antony's Cave.

From Zafarana, on the Red Sea coast road, 120km south of Suez, 250km north of Hurghada, follow the road inland for 30km before turning south for 10km to the monastery. There is no public transport.

MOSES AND THE EXODUS

How much, if any, of the story of the Exodus is historical is a matter of debate. Scholars accept that the Old Testament account was written by persons unknown anything up to 1,000 years after the late second-millenium BC events described. According to biblical tradition, Moses led the Children of Israel from Pi-Ramses in the Delta via the Red Sea, which obediently parted so they could walk across into Sinai. There, God gave Moses the Ten Commandments on top of a mountain, associated with Gebel Musa (Mount Sinai) near St Catherine's Monastery, which also claims possession of the Burning Bush. The Israelites wandered the Sinai for 40 years before finally entering the Promised Land.

The old grain mill, St Antony's Monastery

St Catherine's nestles against Mount Sinai

dressed in a purple robe and holding a staff in his skeletal hand.

Dominating the interior of the monastery is the Church of the Transfiguration. Through the magnificently carved 6th-century inner doors of the narthex you enter the vast nave. At its far end is a gilded iconostasis adorned with large icons of John the Baptist, Mary, Jesus and St Catherine, all 17th-century Cretan work. To the right, behind the iconostasis, is the reliquary said to contain St Catherine's skull and left hand.

In the apse of the church is the 6th-century mosaic of the Transfiguration, one of the finest works of Byzantine art. Its subject is taken from *Matthew 17:1–3*. After Jesus had asked his disciples who they thought he was, he: '...was transfigured before them: and his face

The Greek Orthodox Church, St Catherine's

ST CATHERINE'S MONASTERY
(Deir Sant Katerin)

There are few more dramatic sights in Egypt than the Monastery of St Catherine lying against the flank of Mount Sinai. You approach from what is claimed to be the plain of Raha, where the wandering Israelites worshipped the golden calf, while above you looms the 2,285m mountain where Moses is said to have received the Ten Commandments from God.

Built in about AD530, the monastery is Greek Orthodox, its monks mostly from Crete and Cyprus. Protected by its fortress-like walls and respected by Jews, Christians and Muslims alike for its associations with Moses, St Catherine's Monastery has generally enjoyed the peace and patronage denied to Coptic monasteries, so that it preserves today all the splendour of its Byzantine past.

Outside its gate stands the Charnel House, heaped high with the bones of monks under the inattentive gaze of St Stephen the Porter, a 6th-century monk, did shine as the sun, and his raiment was white as the light'. On either side of the windows above the apse are mosaics of Moses taking off his sandals before the Burning Bush and receiving the Ten Commandments.

A wonderful sampling of the monastery's 5,000 icons is displayed in the new Icon Gallery next to the Library, which has a valuable collection of books and manuscripts, some dating to the 5th century AD.

A winding path climbs up Mount Sinai from behind the monastery. If you wish to have the mountain to yourself, wait until later in the day, but traditionally, visitors leave at 2am, allowing two hours for the climb, in order to reach the summit by sun-up. It can be cold, but the dawn is magnificent and the early morning light superb for photography. The walk is fine for any halfway fit person and the route is easy to follow in the dark. As an alternative, you can hire a camel at the bottom. *In southern Sinai. 443km from Cairo. Buses take 6 hours. There are also flights and tours. Open: daily 9am–12.30pm. Closed: Friday and Sunday. Free.*

SHARM EL SHEIKH, NA'AMA BAY AND RAS MUHAMMAD

Sharm el Sheikh and Na'ama Bay, 7km north, are twin resorts on Sinai's eastern coast. Sharm is growing rapidly and popular with tourists. The limited accommodation is improving. However it is not typical of Egyptian resorts; Na'ama Bay has better reefs and facilities.

From Sharm you can take a boat to Ras Muhammad at the southernmost tip of Sinai, where there are superb views across the Gulf of Suez to the Red Sea mountains and across the Gulf of Aqaba to Saudi Arabia. But most spectacular

are its underwater views, though the sea can be rough out at the reefs, where diving is not really suitable for beginners. Everyone, however, can enjoy the underwater Shark Observatory. *514km southeast from Cairo. Buses, stopping at Sharm and Na'ama Bay, take 6 hours. There are flights to Sharm from Cairo and Hurghada. There is no public transport to the Ras Muhammad national park, although there are boat trips from Sharm el Sheikh. Admission charge.*

SUEZ

Badly affected by the 1967 and 1973 wars with Israel and the sporadic shelling in between, Suez is now a largely rebuilt industrial centre. The Ahmed Hamdi Tunnel, 10km north, is the main route for traffic into Sinai. *134km east of Cairo, reached by trains, buses and service taxis.*

The resort of Sharm el Sheikh

THE SUEZ CANAL

The idea of a canal to link the Red Sea with the Mediterranean is by no means a modern conception. The earliest historically authenticated attempt was made by Necho, a 26th-Dynasty pharaoh, who abandoned the project when an oracle warned that only the Persians would benefit from it. Indeed it was the Persian King Darius I who completed it a century later, in about 500BC.

The first canal ran from the Red Sea to about where present-day Ismailia stands, before turning westwards to Bubastis, near modern Zagazig, to join up with a now vanished arm of the Nile. It was maintained by the Ptolemies and the Romans, but was abandoned by the Arabs.

The present canal, at 167km, is the third longest in the world and the longest without locks. Following its completion in 1869 under the direction of the Frenchman, Ferdinand de Lesseps, Khedive Ismail remarked, 'My country is no longer in Africa; we are now part of Europe. It is therefore natural for us to abandon our former ways and to adopt a new system adapted to our social conditions'.

In fact the khedive was bankrupted by his financial involvement and Egypt

soon fell under British control. Nasser's nationalisation of the foreign-owned Suez Canal Company in 1956 was a reaction to nearly a century of direct or indirect Western rule. This led to the Suez Crisis, an attack on Egypt by Britain, France and Israel, called off after Soviet and American objections. It was one of the most tense and dangerous moments of the Cold War. The 1967 war with Israel closed the canal for eight years, and continual

The Suez Canal – one of the world's most vital passages for trade

shelling of the canal towns during that time caused enormous damage.

In 1975 President Sadat reopened the canal. As many as 90 ships pass through every 24 hours with an average transit time of 15 hours. They carry with them 14 per cent of the world's trade, and the fees they pay are a major income-earner for Egypt.

The Nile Valley

(Cairo to Luxor)

*T*hroughout Egyptian history a distinction has been made between Lower Egypt, which is the land of the Delta, and Upper Egypt, where the desert and mountains encroach upon the Nile valley with its narrow band of cultivation. Lower Egypt, then and now, has been more cosmopolitan, more exposed to foreign influences. From Upper Egypt have come periodic bursts of conservative reaction.

Ancient Memphis and now Cairo stand near the juncture of the Delta and the Nile valley, but the sense of entering Upper Egypt only really begins when you have got beyond Beni Suef, a busy and unattractive town 124km south of Cairo. From this point, you are leaving behind those most impressive monuments of the Old Kingdom at Gîza and Saqqâra. The Nile valley is more associated with later pharaonic periods, though along this first stretch of the river, heavily populated by Copts, there are also several interesting early Christian sites.

ABYDOS

Ancient Abydos was the shrine of Osiris, who as god of the underworld, was also a central figure in Egyptians' notions of resurrection and the afterlife. The Nineteenth-Dynasty New Kingdom pharaoh Seti I, though possessing a mortuary temple in the Theban necropolis, built one here as well. Reacting against Akhenaton's revolution

Atmospheric Abydos, sacred to the memory of Osiris, the god of resurrection

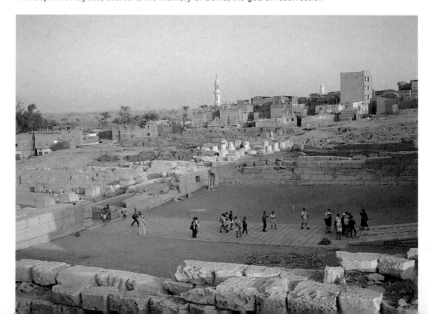

Relief carving on entrance pillar

OSIRIS AND ATON
The cult of Osiris formed part of the orthodox religion of ancient Egypt. The story goes that Osiris, son of Re, was a king who ruled justly and was greatly loved in distant times. Isis was his sister and wife, and Seth was his brother. When Seth killed Osiris and dismembered his body, Isis searched out the pieces and put them together again. Abydos, where Isis found Osiris' head, became a national shrine. Just as she restored him to life in the underworld, so all who followed the Osiris cult would share in the promise of resurrection and eternal life.

The Eighteenth-Dynasty pharaoh, Akhenaton, rejected both the priesthood of Amun at Thebes and the Osiris cult, and was called a heretic. At Amarna, he worshipped instead the Aton, the solar disc, to whom he wrote a hymn, which is found in many of the Amarna tombs.

With the rising sun, goes the hymn, the land awakes in festivity. The trees and plants are green, the birds fly from their nests, the fish in the river leap before its rays, and all the land begins its work. The sun creates the germ in women and the seed in men. It breaths life into all it has created.

in worship and art (see box), Seti was determined to reinstate Egyptian style as it had existed during the Old Kingdom.

The first hypostyle hall was decorated after Seti's death by his son, Ramses II. The more finely carved and coloured work on the walls of the second hypostyle hall (some of the finest reliefs to be seen anywhere in Egypt) were executed during Seti's lifetime. They include profiles of Seti himself, which closely resemble the distinctive features of his mummy at the Museum of Egyptian Antiquities in Cairo.

At the left of the second hypostyle hall is a passageway known as the Gallery of the Kings for its cartouches of Seti's predecessors back to the time of Menes. This has proved invaluable to Egyptologists in determining the correct order of pharaonic succession. Adjacent reliefs show Seti himself and his son, the future Ramses II, revering their ancestors.
600km south of Cairo, on the west bank of

the Nile. 10km southwest of El Balyana, which is 40km northwest of Nag Hammâdi. Several Cairo-Luxor trains stop at El Balyana, from where service taxis run out to Abydos. Alternatively, take a tour or hire a taxi from Luxor, visiting both Abydos and Dendera. These are also covered by some cruises. Open: 7am–6pm. Admission charge.

Detailed wall paintings at Beni Hasan throw light on everyday life in Egypt

ASYÛT

With a population exceeding 250,000, Asyût is the largest town in Upper Egypt. Home to an Islamic university, it was at one time a centre for fundamentalist activity. The local Copts, a third of the city's population, had suffered from sporadic outbursts of violence. Now it is relatively peaceful. *378km south of Cairo. Buses depart from here for the oases of the Western Desert.*

BENI HASAN

A path leads up from the east bank of the Nile to 39 Middle Kingdom tombs cut into the cliff face, though only four are normally open to the public. These tombs belonged to provincial governors and are exceptional for the detail of their paintings which depict agriculture, craft, hunting and sports, along with occasional military scenes, giving a vivid impression of everyday life.
On the east bank of the Nile. 275km south of Cairo and 25km south of El Minya. A taxi from El Minya will take you to the
ferry landing; on your return it can take you on to Amarna. Open: 8am–4pm. Admission charge.

DENDERA

For the ancient Egyptians the goddess of joy and love was Hathor, the cow goddess, whose name means Castle of Horus. As a fertility goddess she suckled Horus, the son of Isis and Osiris, and then lay with him at Edfu in culmination of a great pageant issuing each year from her temple at Dendera.

Every dynasty legitimised itself by identifying with various aspects of the Osiris story, and the Ptolemies were no exception. This **Temple of Hathor** at Dendera is their construction, and later even the Romans took a hand, adding the pylon-shaped façade with its six Hathor-headed columns.

You pass through a succession of halls which become smaller, lower and darker, until you reach the inner sanctuary of the goddess. Normally kept bolted and in darkness, it was opened

Beni Hasan's Middle Kingdom rock tombs are carved into the limestone cliff face

and illuminated by torchlight to allow Hathor's adoration by the pharaoh. This ritual is depicted on wall reliefs inside.

At the New Year, images of the goddess were carried up to the roof where they made contact with the rays of Re – a spiritual emergence from darkness into light. You can retrace the route by climbing the stairways from within the temple, their walls incised with reliefs illustrating the procession. Near the base of the west stairway is the New Year Chapel. On its ceiling is a magnificent relief of Nut, the sky goddess, giving birth to the sun whose rays illuminate Hathor.

On the roof is the elegant kiosk where Hathor was exposed to the sun's revivifying force, while above the stairwells are the twin chapels of Osiris, their decorations including a zodiac (though the original has been removed to the Louvre).

Colossal reliefs on the outside rear wall of the temple show Caesarion, son of Julius Caesar, with his mother, the great Cleopatra and last of the Ptolemies, making offerings to a head of Hathor.

618km south of Cairo, on the west bank of the Nile. 4km west of Qena. From the train station here you can take a taxi or carriage to the temple. Alternatively, take a tour or hire a taxi from Luxor, visiting both Dendera and Abydos, which are also sometimes covered by cruises. Temple open: 7am–6pm. Admission charge.

EL MINYA

Within easy reach of Beni Hasan and Amarna, El Minya, which has a large Christian community, has unfortunately taken over from Asyût as the centre for unrest, suffering from sporadic outbursts of violence. Nevertheless its warm and friendly population enjoys promenading along its winding riverside corniche, while amid overgrown gardens stand charming villas, once the homes of Greek and Egyptian cotton magnates. *On the west bank of the Nile. 247km south of Cairo.*

MONASTERIES ALONG THE NILE

BURNT MONASTERY (Deir el Muharraq)

Unusually, this flourishing Coptic monastery is not far off in the desert but just within the cultivation. By tradition this marks the southernmost point in the flight of the Holy Family. Here, it is said, Joseph heard the angel's words as recorded in St Matthew's Gospel: 'Arise, and take the young child and his mother, and go into the land of Israel.' A church dating back at least to the 8th century and dedicated to the Virgin, El Adra, stands over the cave where the Holy Family supposedly stayed. Next to it is a 12th-century keep. Annually during the week of 21 June, upwards of 50,000 people attend the Feast of the Consecration of the Church of the Virgin.

On the west bank of the Nile. About 30km south of the ferry crossing for Amarna, 80km south of El Minya, and 40km north of Asyût. A visit by taxi could be included in a tour of Beni Hasan and Amarna. For details on visiting Coptic monasteries, see page 179.

WHITE MONASTERY (Deir el Abyad)

As you follow the road out from Sohâg you see a startling sight – at the edge of the cultivation, with its back against the hills of the desert plateau, stands what seems to be an intact Egyptian temple. The White Monastery is the most remarkable instance of resemblance between Coptic and pharaonic architecture.

Massive white limestone walls slope inwards and are finished off with a cavetto cornice of white marble. Inside is an enormous basilical church. To call it a monastery is misleading, for the ruins of that once vast structure housing over 2,000 monks now lie beneath the mounds of debris outside. The surviving building is in fact a fortified monastery church built in about AD440 by St Shenute, whose *moulid* is celebrated here during the week leading up to 14 July.

The nave is ruinous – much of the damage was caused by Mamelukes fleeing Napoleon's troops in 1798. Nevertheless, the proportions and the broken columns of marble and black granite make a noble impression. What was the sanctuary has been bricked off to form a complete church, its apses arranged as a trefoil, with 12th-century paintings adorning their semidomes. *Sohâg is 470km south of Cairo. From there a taxi can take you the 5km west to the White Monastery. Open: daily 7am–6pm; all night during the* moulid. *Free.*

TELL EL AMARNA

When the Eighteenth-Dynasty pharaoh Akhenaton broke with the worship of Amun at Thebes in favour of the sun disc Aton (see page 83), he founded his new capital Akhetaton ('Resting Place of the Disc') at the place now called Tell el Amarna, or simply Amarna. The city was abandoned after the deaths of Akhenaton and his beautiful queen Nefertiti. Thebes again became capital and a compliant Tutankhamun was persuaded to reinstate the worship of Amun.

Only the merest traces of palaces, temples and houses remain in this great sand-filled crescent between the Nile and the cliffs of the Eastern Desert. The cliff face tombs are most worth visiting for the view back over the plain. There is a lonely and melancholy beauty to

Amarna, but for its paintings, reliefs and sculptures you must visit the Museum of Egyptian Antiquities in Cairo.

On the east bank of the Nile. 314km south of Cairo and 67km south of El Minya. From El Minya, take a taxi to the west bank ferry landing and cross over to the village of El Till. The site lies behind the village. Access is unrestricted and free. At the village you can hire donkeys or a tractor to visit the tombs, 4km east. Open: 7am–5pm. Admission charge.

Relief carvings (right) at Tell el Amarna's rock tombs (below)

THE RIVER OF LIFE

When you rush by road or rail the impression escapes you, and from the air all you can see is a dimensionless ribbon. But when you sail for days along the Nile there is the clear sense that you are travelling along a valley.

The Nile cuts through rock and cliffs close on either side. Sometimes the valley walls are distant and the sense is momentarily lost, but then the river swings back against the rock and reminds you of the eons it has spent carving its passage. Perhaps valley is misleading; this is more a groove, a broad canyon. It is a cut through sandstone and limestone, filled with mud from Africa.

Downriver from Luxor there are shallows and mudbanks and low lying fields where land and river mingle; there are reed hides, hunters and fishermen, animals grazing on half-sunken islands, and sometimes, instead of mud brick villages, scatterings of palm-roofed dwellings like seasonal encampments, tentative, suggesting the earliest settlements along the Nile.

It is godly to cruise the Nile through Egypt. Before the roads and railways there was only this river, and as the pharaohs and their people sailed upon it and watched their world unroll, it cannot have helped making a special impression on them all.

The echoing silence of the deserts spoke of the void beyond the grave. But here along the river was the rhythm of bright green fields perpetually tender, distant figures absorbed in their patch, fishermen poling through the reeds like spiky water insects.

You are gliding along the artery of life itself. It is like the most beautiful murals in the ancient tombs, too sweet not to carry into eternity.

Africa's longest river continues to influence the lives of Egyptians today, much as it has always done

Luxor

*T*he name Luxor is loosely applied by travellers to include three distinct places: the town of Luxor, with a population of 100,000, on the east bank of the Nile; the village of Karnak and its immense temple 4km north on the same bank; and the Theban necropolis on the west bank of the river opposite Luxor and Karnak.

At the height of its glory during the 18th and 19th Dynasties, Thebes covered all of what is now Luxor and Karnak and may have had a population as high as one million. Earlier, in Middle Kingdom times, its most important god had been Amun. When the Theban princes drove the alien Hyksos out of Lower Egypt and reunited the country, Thebes became capital of the New Kingdom and Amun, Egypt's national god.

Apart from its military prowess, Thebes was also strategically situated between the agriculturally rich Delta and gold-rich Nubia. It is tempting to believe that the great pharaohs of the New Kingdom also responded to the beauty and never-failing fertility of the surrounding landscape. It did inspire them to build, sometimes sensitively, sometimes grandiosely, and Thebes became the focus of an architectural activity so magnificent, and still well enough preserved, that it can lay just claim to being the world's greatest outdoor museum.

On the east bank, highlights include

Right: Obelisk at the entrance to the Temple of Amun at Karnak

LUXOR AND THEBES

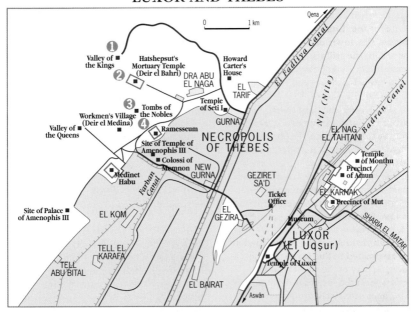

VISITING THE WEST BANK

The first thing you should do when landing on the west bank of the Nile is to buy tickets for all the tombs and temples of the Theban necropolis that you want to visit that day. You will not be allowed into the sites without a ticket. Some tombs are likely to be closed. You will find out which ones only when buying your tickets, so have alternative choices in mind. Do not buy too many, as they are valid only on the day of issue. If you find you have time to visit further sites,

there is another ticket kiosk near the Colossi of Memnon.

There are two landing stages, the southern one where you can hire a taxi, the northern one where you buy entrance tickets for the tombs and temples. Hire a taxi first, then buy your tickets. The two ticket offices are open daily from 6am; the tombs and temples from 6am to 5pm in summer, 4pm in winter. No ticket is needed for the Colossi of Memnon. All other sights charge admission.

the Temple of Luxor in Luxor itself and the Temple of Amun in Karnak, scene of the sound and light show. The west bank highlights are covered by the taxi

tour of the Theban necropolis on pages 104–5, which includes the Valley of the Kings, Hatshepsut's mortuary temple and the Ramesseum.

COLOSSI OF MEMNON

The mortuary temple of Amenophis III has vanished and all that remains are the two famous colossi which once guarded its outer gates. They are, in fact, gigantic statues of the enthroned Amenophis himself, 19.5m high. At one time they wore the royal crown and were even higher.

The one on the right (north) was shattered by an earthquake in 27BC and later repaired; for nearly 200 years thereafter it would often emit a musical note as the sun rose over the eastern mountains. Greek and Roman tourists, including the emperor Hadrian in AD130, camped overnight to witness the phenomenon and carved their names into the colossi's legs.

On the west bank in the southern part of the necropolis. 3.5km from the Nile.

> ### 'WONDERFUL THINGS!'
> About his discovery of Tutankhamun's tomb, Howard Carter wrote: 'Details of the room within emerged slowly from the mist, strange animals, statues, and gold – everywhere the glint of gold. For the moment – an eternity it must have seemed to the others standing by – I was struck dumb with amazement, and when Lord Carnarvon, unable to stand the suspense any longer, enquired anxiously "Can you see anything?" it was all I could do to get out the words, "Yes, wonderful things".'

HATSHEPSUT'S MORTUARY TEMPLE (Deir el Bahri)

Hatshepsut's father, the Eighteenth-Dynasty pharaoh Tuthmosis I, was the first to seek greater security for his mummified body by having a tomb dug in the Valley of the Kings. Hatshepsut followed his example, but before and ever after her burial the appropriate ceremonies were to be held at her mortuary temple (see page 105). Early Christians later used it as a monastery, which is why it is often known as Deir el Bahri, the Northern Monastery.

The temple has three terraces linked by ramps. The Lower Terrace was a garden with myrrh trees and fountains, as though a foretaste of that life which endures in the desert of the other world. Within the right colonnade at the rear of the terrace this theme is continued in delicate reliefs depicting an idealised country life. At the rear of the Middle Terrace, reliefs to the left, along the Punt Colonnade, show Egyptians who

Colossi of Memnon, survivors of 3,000 years

Hatshepsut's Mortuary Temple (Deir el Bahri) rises out of the desert plain

have sailed south along the African coast to obtain myrrh trees for the temple being greeted by the chief of Punt and his extraordinarily corpulent wife. Reliefs along the Birth Colonnade to the right announce Hatshepsut's divine parentage, her father as Amun sitting opposite her mother Ahmosis, who is then led to the birth chamber.

As a woman pharaoh, Hatshepsut was eager to underline the legitimacy of her rule, especially as it was being challenged by her stepson and nominal co-ruler, the future Tuthmosis III. When he finally came to the throne, following her death, he resentfully defaced her images here on the pillars of the Birth Colonnade and elsewhere,

while preserving his own. The Upper Terrace, which is still undergoing restoration, is closed.

On the west bank, at the north end of the necropolis. 6km from the river. See box on page 91 for ticket details.

HOWARD CARTER'S HOUSE (Qasr Carter)

On a barren hill overlooking the road which rises towards the Valley of the Kings is the large domed house where Howard Carter lived during the years before and after his discovery of Tutankhamun's tomb.

At the north end of the necropolis. 1km north of Seti I's mortuary temple and 5km from the river. It is closed to the public.

Karnak

*T*he Karnak site covers a huge area. The precinct of Amun in fact encloses several temples, but most people will be content to walk through the biggest of these, the Temple of Amun, whose Hypostyle Hall alone is large enough to contain both St Paul's Cathedral in London and St Peter's Church in Rome.

One dynasty after another added to the Temple of Amun, so that from its founding during the Middle Kingdom to the building of its outermost or First Pylon during the 25th Dynasty, 1,300 years elapsed. The Asian conquests of Tuthmosis III and Ramses II brought New Kingdom Egypt to the peak of power and prosperity. The great god Amun also received his share, so that his temple soon controlled perhaps as much as a fifth of Egypt's workforce and owned nearly a third of its land.

Something of this story is told during the sound and light show which leads you briskly through part of the Temple of Amun and deposits you in the grandstand overlooking the Sacred Lake.

By day you have more of a chance to get your bearings. A processional way lined with ram-headed sphinxes leads into the temple. They represent Amun, and between the forelegs of each is a diminutive figure of the god's servant, Ramses II. The First Pylon was built 600 years later. At 43m high it is the largest at Karnak and nearly twice the size of the entrance pylon at the Temple of Luxor. A succession of pylons funnel you towards the sanctuary of the god.

Passing through the Second Pylon you enter the Hypostyle Hall, the Nineteenth-Dynasty work of Seti I and Ramses II. Its forest of columns is one of the most spectacular sights in Egypt. Each column is so massive that it takes the outstretched arms of six people to

Ram statue, Temple of Amun

encircle one. The entire hall was once roofed over.

An obelisk raised by Tuthmosis I stands in the small court between the Third and Fourth Pylons. Between the Fourth and Fifth Pylons stood two magnificent obelisks of Tuthmosis I's daughter, Hatshepsut. One has snapped in half; the upper portion lies at the northwest corner of the Sacred Lake where you can examine its fine hieroglyphic inscriptions. The other remains in place and at 29.5m is the tallest obelisk in Egypt.

You will notice two pink granite pillars carved with lilies on one side and papyrus flowers on the other, the traditional symbols of Upper and Lower

The overpowering Hypostyle Hall of the Temple of Amun, with its gigantic columns

On the east bank. 4km north of Luxor. Open: daily 6am–5.30pm (6.30pm in summer). Admission charge. Sound and Light shows are daily at 8pm and 10pm in the following languages: Monday – English, French; Tuesday – French, English; Wednesday – English, German; Thursday – Arabic, English; Friday – French, English; Saturday – English, French; Sunday – French, German. Programme subject to change. Admission charge.

Egypt. Past these is the Sanctuary of the Sacred Boats, built in the time of Alexander the Great to replace the original.

Along the south flank of the Temple of Amun is the Sacred Lake where the god's sacred boats took part in various ceremonies culminating in the annual Opet festival when he sailed upriver to the Temple of Luxor. At its northwest corner, by part of Hatshepsut's obelisk, is a gigantic scarab dedicated by Amenophis III to the rising sun.

LUXOR MUSEUM

The museum contains a small but carefully selected number of beautifully displayed exhibits. Graeco-Roman, Coptic and Islamic artefacts are included, but the overwhelming emphasis is on the pharaonic period.

There are a few items from Tutankhamun's tomb, including a funerary bed, model boats and a golden cow's head. The other contents of his tomb are all in the Museum of Egyptian Antiquities in Cairo. Reliefs of Akhenaton and Nefertiti worshipping Aton, and scenes of their palace life are also displayed.

Most outstanding, however, are the black basalt and pink granite statues and busts of jug-eared Sesostris III of the Twelfth Dynasty and of the Eighteenth-Dynasty pharaohs Tuthmosis III, Amenophis II and Amenophis III. The craftsmanship is superb, and you can feel the sculptors' enjoyment of working with the graceful curves of crowns, necks and waists.

On the east bank, on Sharia Nahr el Nil.
1km north of the Temple of Luxor. Open:
daily 9am–1pm and 4–9pm in winter;
9am–1pm and 5–10pm in summer.
Admission charge.

LUXOR TEMPLE

Until the end of the 19th century, when excavations began, almost the whole of Luxor village stood within and on top of this debris-filled temple. Only the mosque of Abu Haggag was allowed to remain perched on top of its walls. Unlike Karnak, which was built over a long period of time, the Temple of Luxor is largely the work of the Eighteenth-Dynasty pharaoh Amenophis III. With him began the fashion for gigantism that broadcasts the imperial pretensions of

Cow bust, Museum of Antiquities

New Kingdom Egypt.

It was Ramses II, however, who later built the entrance pylons and the great court beyond. In front of the pylons he placed six colossal statues of himself, only three of which remain. Of the two obelisks he erected here, one was given to the French by Mohammed Ali and now stands in the Place de la Concorde in Paris. Incised on the pylons are scenes of the battle of Kadesh in Syria, which Ramses claimed as a victory against the Hittites, though he was lucky to escape from it with his life. The vertical grooves on the pylons were for supporting flagstaffs.

Numerous colossi of Ramses stand around the great court, his wife Nefertari knee-high at his side. On the far right-hand wall a relief shows the exterior of the temple, complete with colossi and obelisks, and banners waving from the pylons.

From here, you enter the imposing colonnade of Amenophis III. On the right-hand wall are reliefs dating from the reign of Tutankhamun illustrating the Opet festival, an annual fertility rite, during which Amun sailed from Karnak for a conjugal reunion with his wife Mut, who resided at the Temple of Luxor with their son Khonsu. The Court of Amenophis leads to his Hypostyle Hall with reliefs on its far walls showing his coronation by the gods.

These in turn lead on to the Sanctuary of the Sacred Boat of Amun, corresponding to the one at Karnak. Its inner chamber was rebuilt during the time of Alexander the Great. On the outside wall facing the river is a relief of a pharaonic-looking Alexander offering gifts to Amun who is in a state of presumably festive erection.

Returning back through the temple and emerging again at the pylons, you notice the avenue of sphinxes that once led all the way to Karnak.

On the east bank, on Sharia Nahr el Nil at the centre of Luxor. Open: daily 6am–9pm in winter; 6am–10pm in summer.
Admission charge, reduced after 6pm, when the temple is beautifully floodlit.

Statue of Ramses II at Luxor Temple

Relief carving in the Temple of Ramses II

MEDÎNET HABU (Mortuary Temple of Ramses III)

Ramses III's great mortuary temple is usually known as Medînet Habu, 'town of Habu'. During the Coptic period there was indeed a town of some size here, while part of the temple was used as a church.

Modelled closely on the Ramesseum, which had been built less than a century earlier, the temple of Ramses III is much better preserved, and is second in size only to the Temple of Amun at Karnak. It was, however, to prove the last major architectural work of the pharaonic period. During the remainder of the Twentieth Dynasty, Egypt's fortunes were on the wane.

You enter the site by a gatehouse, which, judging from the reliefs on the walls of its upper storey, served as a resort where the pharaoh could amuse himself with the harem women. Straight ahead is the First Pylon which is worth climbing to gain an overall impression of temple layout, the pylons, columns and chambers becoming smaller and smaller as you gaze towards the sanctuary.

This was not only a mortuary temple, but also a royal residence. The First Court was the scene of ceremonies and entertainments, the pharaoh perhaps making appearances at the window in the left-hand wall which was also the palace façade. During the Ptolemaic and Roman periods, the Second Court was filled with houses and a church – the octagonal base of its font can be seen on the left.

Beyond this are three hypostyle halls leading to the sanctuary which once contained Amun's boat. Left off the Second Hypostyle Hall is the funerary chamber of Ramses III with depictions of Thoth inscribing the pharaoh's name on the sacred tree.

If you now go back through the First Pylon and turn left, you can walk round to the outside wall of the temple to see its famous panoramic relief. This shows the attempted invasion of Egypt by the Sea Peoples, a coalition of northerners who had already overrun the Hittite empire in Anatolia (present-day Turkey) and Syria. They are shown arriving in ships and overland by ox-cart, bringing their families and all their belongings, attacking the Delta, and being repulsed by Ramses.

An inscription graphically describes the outcome: 'A net was prepared for them to ensnare them, those who entered into the rivermouths being confined and fallen within it, pinioned in their places, butchered and their corpses hacked up.'

On the west bank, at the southern end of the necropolis. 5km from the river.

Vivid bas-reliefs in the Tombs of the Nobles depict scenes of everyday life

NOBLES' TOMBS

Hundreds of nobles' tombs have been found in the Theban Necropolis. Two of the most interesting, those of Ramose and Sennufer, are described on page 105. Also worth visiting, if you have the time, are the tombs of Rekhmire, Menna, Nakht, Userhat and Khaemhat.
On the west bank near, and sometimes under, the village of Sheikh Abd el Gurna. 5km from the river. They are signposted from the Ramesseum.

THE RAMESSEUM

See page 105.
On the west bank, at the centre of the Theban Necropolis. 5km from the river.

SETI I'S MORTUARY TEMPLE

If you are unable to see Seti's exquisite reliefs at Abydos (see pages 82–3), then you should visit his temple here. Some of the reliefs are best seen from above, so you leap goat-like after the resident guide, from lintel to broken lintel.
On the west bank, at the north end of the Theban necropolis en route to the Valley of the Kings. 4km from the river.

TICKET DETAILS
See box on page 91 for ticket details for Medînet Habu, the Nobles' Tombs, the Ramesseum and Seti I's Mortuary Temple.

Valley of the Kings

*L*eaving the cultivation behind, the road climbs towards the Valley of the Kings, an oven of white sand and sun containing 62 tombs, almost all belonging to pharaohs of the 18th, 19th and 20th Dynasties (1570–1090BC). The tombs were cut into the soft limestone by workmen living at Deir el Medina. Construction and decoration began as soon as a pharaoh came to the throne and followed a similar pattern in all the tombs. Three corridors lead to an antechamber giving on to a main hall with a sunken floor for receiving the sarcophagus.

The recurrent theme of the decorations has the dead pharaoh, absorbed in the sun god, sailing through the underworld at night in a boat, with enemies and dangers to be avoided along the way. Inscriptions from the *Book of the Dead* provide instructions for charting the course. After this nocturnal voyage the naked body of the sky goddess Nut gives birth each morning to the sun.

It is thought the dramatic discovery of Tutankhamun's tomb in 1922 was the last and that all the tombs have now been found. Most are of little interest except to scholars and are closed to the public. Only tombs 2, 6, 8, 9, 11, 16, 17, 34, 35, 57 and 62 have electric lighting, and not all of these are always open. Most visitors will be content to see the tombs of Tutankhamun (62), Ramses VI (9), Seti I (17) and Ramses IV (2). Even some of these may be closed when you visit.

TOMB 2: RAMSES IV
(20th Dynasty)
The New Kingdom was already in decline when this tomb was cut. Its decorations are of inferior quality, but the patterns of bright colours against an overall background of white, and the excellent lighting, contribute towards a favourable impression. There is much

Ptolemaic and Coptic graffiti throughout, particularly to the right of the entrance where two haloed saints raise their arms in prayer. The ceiling of the sarcophagus chamber is decorated with the goddess Nut. The huge pink granite sarcophagus is covered with texts and magical scenes, while Nephthys and Isis on the lid were meant to protect the body – which was, nevertheless, hijacked in antiquity and never found.

TOMB 9: RAMSES VI
(20th Dynasty)
Constructed for Ramses V, this tomb originally ended after three corridors but

---

The Valley of the Kings is on the west bank, 7km from the Nile. It is reached by a steeply rising road which curves round the northern end of the Theban Necropolis. The hardy can leave the Valley of the Kings by a mountain track which starts between Tombs 10 and 16 and divides at the top of the ridge, one arm descending to the left to Hatshepsut's mortuary temple, the other continuing straight ahead along the ridge until it descends at Deir el Medina. For ticket details see box page 91.

VALLEY OF THE KINGS

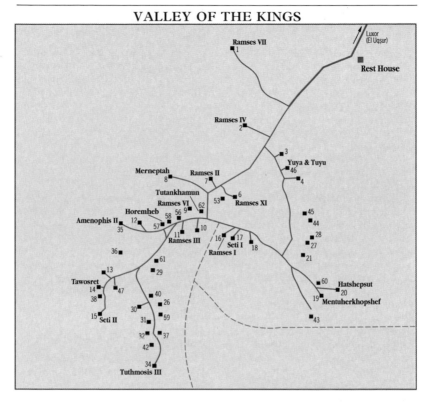

was later extended to double its length. The colouring remains fresh throughout. The pillared end-chamber contains fragments of the huge granite sarcophagus. A magnificent painting of Nut in duplicate adorns its vaulted ceiling.

TOMB 17: SETI I (19th Dynasty)

At 100m, the Tomb of Seti I is the longest in the valley. Its reliefs are wonderfully preserved and beautifully executed. On the left wall of the entrance corridor, Seti is greeted by falcon-headed Re-Herakhte, god of the morning sun. The next two corridors are decorated with instructions from the *Book of the Dead* on how to navigate the underworld. In the three chambers beyond, Seti is shown with various deities. These motifs are then repeated in the second half of the tomb.

Finally there is the burial chamber with astronomical figures on the vaulted ceiling. In the small chamber to the right, the sky goddess Nut is shown in the form of a cow.

TOMB 62: TUTANKHAMUN (18th Dynasty)

This tomb is described on page 104.

VALLEY OF THE QUEENS

This valley contains over 70 tombs of queens, princes and princesses of the 18th, 19th and 20th Dynasties, though only four are open. Unlike the pharaohs, however, these lesser royal figures were not gods and so their tombs are more humble affairs.

Tomb 66: Queen Nefertari (19th Dynasty)

Nefertari was the wife of Ramses II and is celebrated in stone at Abu Simbel and elsewhere. Her tomb, long closed owing to damage caused by salt deposits, has been marvellously restored and recently reopened. It is by far the finest in the valley, the wall paintings exquisitely drawn and vividly coloured. Admission is restricted to 200 people a day, and there is a premium admission charge.

Tomb 55: Prince Amun-Her-Khopshef (20th Dynasty)

A smallpox epidemic towards the end of Ramses III's reign killed off several of his sons. In the hall at the bottom of the entrance steps there is a painting showing the pharaoh introducing one of them, Amun-Her-Khopshef, to the gods. The paintings throughout this tomb are fresh and finely executed. At the centre of the burial chamber there is a sarcophagus in human, or rather mummy form. The bones of a six-month-old foetus are displayed in a glass case.

Tomb 44: Prince Khaemweset (20th Dynasty)

Belonging to another son of Ramses III who fell victim to smallpox, the decorations of this tomb are similar to those of Tomb 55 and are more easily observed as there is no foetus here to draw the crowds.

A detail from a tomb in the Valley of the Queens

Tomb 52: Queen Titi (20th Dynasty)

Though inscriptions describe Titi as a daughter, wife and mother of pharaohs, it is not known to which pharaohs these refer. The paintings are badly faded and damaged. The tomb is arranged like a cross, a corridor leading to a central chamber off which are three smaller chambers, left, right and ahead. In the small chamber on the right, Titi is shown with a tree-goddess and Hathor as a cow. She also appears on the left and right walls of the small chamber ahead.

> **The Valley of the Queens** is on the west bank, at the southern end of the Theban Necropolis, 5km from the river. See page 91 for ticket details.

WORKMEN'S VILLAGE
(Deir el Medina)

Deir el Medina means 'monastery of the town', for the workmen's village and the small Ptolemaic temple just north of it were occupied by monks during the early years of Christianity. During the New Kingdom, this was home to the highly skilled artisans who cut and decorated the royal tombs in the Valley of the Kings. The remains of over 70 houses are evident, their mud-brick walls rising on stone foundations along straight and narrow alleys. They had a second storey or at least a living area on the roof, reached by outside stairs.

They also fashioned their own tombs, but unlike those of the nobles who decorated their tombs with vivid scenes of everyday life, these workmen more often borrowed motifs from the Valley of the Kings. Over the tomb entrance they would build a man-sized pyramid. Usually two or three of these tombs are open.

The tomb of Sennedjem (Tomb 1) has a vaulted chamber down steep steps, in which there is a finely painted relief of a funeral feast and also a nice cameo touch of a cat killing a snake under the sacred tree. The tomb of Peshedu (Tomb 3) shows him praying beneath the tree of regeneration.

On the west bank at the southern end of the Theban Necropolis. 4.5km from the river.

See page 91 for ticket details.

One of the many man-sized pyramid tombs at Deir el Medina

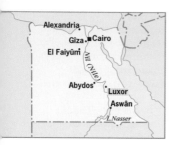

The Theban Necropolis by Taxi

Allow 4 hours to complete this highlight tour of the necropolis. See page 91 for a map of the tour.

Begin at the west bank ticket office. Drive across the cultivation and up through the desert hills into the Valley of the Kings.

1 TUTANKHAMUN'S TOMB

Discovered by Howard Carter in 1922, this is the only tomb in the Valley of the Kings to have been found with its contents intact. Owing to the pharaoh's early death at 19 (he had

ascended to the throne at the age of 12), the tomb is small and was hurriedly decorated. Its treasures have been removed to Cairo. All that remains here now is the open sarcophagus. Within it lies the outermost of the three gold sarcophagi, and, unseen within that, the mummy of Tutankhamun himself. The right wall shows the coffin transported on a sled. The centre wall shows, from right to left, the opening of the mouth ceremony, Tutankhamun sacrificing to the sky goddess Nut, and the young pharaoh with his *ka* before Osiris. On the left wall is the sun god's boat. The Tomb of Seti I should also be visited. For details of this and other tombs in the Valley of the Kings, see pages 100–1.

Arrange for your driver to meet you at Deir el Bahri while you walk (or take a donkey) over the path rising out of the Valley of the Kings between tombs 10 and 16. At the top of the ridge, turn left, then descend to Hatshepsut's temple.

Fallen head of Ramses II

2 HATSHEPSUT'S MORTUARY TEMPLE (Deir el Bahri)

See box on page 91 for information on tickets and taxis.

Apart from Cleopatra, Hatshepsut was the only woman to rule as pharaoh, and she immortalised her reign by brilliantly setting her temple against a pyramid-shaped cliff face to create a powerful yet elegant ensemble (see pages 92–3).

Immediately south is the village of Sheikh Abd el Gurna, built upon a hillside dotted with nobles' tombs.

3 TOMBS OF THE NOBLES

Unlike the tombs in the Valley of the Kings, the nobles' tombs strike a personal note. Others are listed on page 99.

Sennufer's Tomb

This Eighteenth-Dynasty mayor of Thebes was probably also chief vintner to Amenophis II, and you wonder whether his tomb is not his last laugh on that theme. Vines and grapes are painted on wobbly ceilings, walls and pillars as though you and Sennufer had had one drink too many.

Ramose's Tomb

Ramose was vizier to Amenophis IV and as you follow these exquisitely carved reliefs round the walls you witness one of the great revolutions in Egyptian history. Begun in classical style, the reliefs continue in the Amarna style, because Amenophis IV had become Akhenaton and changed the art and religion of his country.

South from the village is the Ramesseum.

4 RAMESSEUM

This huge mortuary temple of Ramses II is such a confusing ruin that it is enough to look at his gigantic fallen statue. Into its mouth Shelley put these ironic words from his poem *Ozymandias*: 'Look on my works, ye Mighty, and despair!'

Alternatively, or additionally, visit Medînet Habu (allowing 30 minutes). Its temple of Ramses III is more complete than the Ramesseum.

Driving south from the Ramesseum and then east, you can pause at the Colossi of Memnon before continuing on to the ferry landing.

Death mask of Tutankhamun

The Nile Valley

(Luxor to Aswan)

*T*he valley of the Nile narrows south of Luxor and the desert impinges more closely on either side. The ribbon of cultivation seems more fragile, its colours more delicate, and the debt that life in Egypt owes to the river becomes more striking. You notice this especially on the east bank beyond Edfu where a narrow strip of palms and cultivation sometimes vanishes altogether.

Like a string of citadels extending Alexandrian power towards Nubia, the Ptolemies built temples along the Nile at Esna, Edfu and Kom Ombo. At Silsileh, 40km south of Edfu, the Nile passes through a defile. Now there are only hills on either side, but there was probably once a cataract. The bedrock of Egypt changes here from limestone to the harder sandstone used in almost all New Kingdom and Ptolemaic temple building. During the reign of Ramses II, the Silsileh quarries were worked by no fewer than 3,000 men for the Ramesseum alone.

EDFU

The present town of Edfu, on the west bank of the Nile (see page 115), is spread upon the mound of the ancient city of Djeba, which the Ptolemies – who identified the Greek sun god Apollo with Horus – called *Apollinopolis Magna*. Here, according to myth, Horus avenged the murder of his father Osiris by defeating Seth in titanic combat. To mark this triumph of good over evil, a succession of shrines was built here from earliest dynastic times, culminating with what is the best preserved ancient monument in Egypt, the Ptolemaic Temple of Horus on the west side of town.
115km south of Luxor.

Temple of Horus

Until the latter part of the 19th century the temple was almost entirely covered by debris and houses stood upon its roof. Only its enormous pylon rose clear above the habitations. Even today the surrounding town obscures your view of it from any distance. And so the impression is all the greater when you arrive at the site and suddenly see the temple all at once.

Statue of the god Horus (Haroeris) in the form of a falcon

One of many falcon statues at the temple

Its huge size strikes you with amazement, and its near-perfect state of preservation makes it seem like a recent leftover from some Hollywood spectacular.

Construction began in 237BC and continued for 25 years, though some of the decorations were not completed for another 150 years after that. Despite his New Kingdom appearance, the giant pharaoh shown braining his enemies on the pylon façade is Ptolemy XII Neos Dionysos, who died in 51BC. He built also at Dendera and was the father of Cleopatra.

You pass across a vast colonnaded courtyard towards a pair of huge granite falcon-Horuses, one standing, the other headless and fallen in the dust, which guard the entrance to the temple chambers. These chambers become ever smaller, ever darker, and lead finally to the sanctuary of the god, weirdly illuminated through three small apertures in the ceiling by a dim green light.

The reliefs on the inner walls of the sanctuary correspond to those at Dendera, and show a Ptolemaic king entering the sanctuary and worshipping

Pillars inside the Temple of Horus, Egypt's best preserved temple of its time

Horus, Hathor and the king's own deified parents. His pendant arms indicate an attitude of reverence.

A sensuously-shaped relief of Nut decorates the ceiling of the New Year Chapel which is to the left as you emerge from the sanctuary. Near by, staircases lead up to the roof, with representations along their walls showing, as at Dendera, how the residing deity was carried up to the roof to be impregnated by the sun.

Western outskirts of Edfu, 2km from the Nile. A carriage can be hired at the quay-side. You can walk in 20 minutes from the service taxi depot near the bridge or the train station on the east bank of the river, though private taxis are available from either. Open: daily 7am–6pm in summer; 7am–4pm in winter. Admission charge.

The temple dedicated to Khnum, the ram-headed god who fashioned men out of the Nile mud

ESNA

Like other towns along the Nile, Esna was, until the end of the 19th century, a port of call for camel caravans crossing the desert from the Sudan (see page 115). It is still something of a merchant town and weaving centre, with elegant old houses along the west bank of the Nile and in the streets behind. Several of these houses are decorated with fine brickwork and *mashrabiyya* screens. There is also a small and picturesque covered market street, where lengths of fabric are sold or made up into clothing.

Temple of Khnum

Only partly excavated, the Temple of Khnum squats in a pit alongside the covered market street. Here you still have some impression of how many ancient monuments appeared until Egyptologists went to work on them in the 19th century, for the rear of the temple remains buried beneath a mound of debris which is partly built over with houses.

Ram-headed Khnum was the patron god of the Cataracts who fashioned man from the mud on his potter's wheel. Ptolemy VI rebuilt the temple in the mid-second century BC over the ruins of earlier structures, though almost all that the excavators have laid bare is the hypostyle hall begun two centuries later during the reign of the Roman emperor Claudius.

The roof of the hall is still intact,

TEMPLE FESTIVITIES

As impressive as the ancient temples seem today, they are no more than empty shells, stripped of their furniture, their decoration, their ceremonies, and indeed their liveliness. But an Edfu text describes how things once were, when the populace of the city could participate in the great festivals that took place at the Temple of Horus: 'Its supplies are more abundant than the sands of the shore. Wine flows in the districts like the inundation pouring from the source of the Nile. Myrrh is on the fire and incense can be smelt a mile away. It is decorated with faïence, shining with natron, decked with flowers and herbs. The priests and officiants are dressed in fine linen, and the king's party is made fine in its regalia. Its young people are drunk, its populace is happy, its young girls are beautiful to see. Jollity is all around it, carnival is in all its districts, and there is no sleep until dawn.'

supported by 24 columns bearing painted capitals in 16 different styles. This is what you come to see, and it is best to stand here, slowly revolving, looking upwards at the myriad palm and

Baubles, bangles and beads

composite plant capitals, arranged without order or symmetry, but with the most pleasing effect, as though you were standing among trees, admiring the subtle and powerful architecture of a forest.

The last cartouche carved on the temple walls is that of the Roman emperor Decius, who reigned from AD249 to 251. He began a series of increasingly severe persecutions against the new Christian religion and decreed that all its followers must sacrifice to the Roman gods or suffer death.

Testimony to his lack of success in Egypt is to be found in the forecourt of the temple where there are several blocks from an early Christian church, including a lion-headed font carved from an ancient block bearing fine hieroglyphics on the reverse.

Esna is 55km south of Luxor. The Temple of Khnum is at the centre of Esna, a few streets west of the Nile landing stage. It is a 10-minute walk from the service taxi depot; carriages are available from the more distant train station. Open: daily 6am–5.30pm in winter; 6am–6.30pm in summer. Admission charge.

KOM OMBO

The reclaimed land on the east bank around Kom Ombo supports a large Nubian population displaced from their homeland by the rising waters of Lake Nasser. Irrigation keeps the desert at bay, and the fields give rich harvests of wheat and sugar cane. A few kilometres away from the village with its sugar refinery is the Ptolemaic temple.
164km south of Luxor, 46km north of Aswân.

Temple of Sobek and Haroeris

The temple stands on a low promontory overlooking the Nile. Its elevation, its seclusion and the river flowing by below, make it a magical place to visit, especially from a felucca or cruise boat. Its relationship to the landscape reminds you of a Greek temple, but though built by Greeks and added to by Romans, the style is pharaonic. As with all Ptolemaic temples, the intention was to reconcile the Egyptian priesthood to foreign rule from Alexandria.

The naos or inner temple was begun by Ptolemy VI Philometor, who built also at Esna, while the hypostyle hall and the pronaos were built by Ptolemy XII Neos Dionysos, whose reliefs adorn the pylon at Edfu. The outer court and the now vanished pylon were added during the time of Augustus.

This is a symmetrical twin temple, the left side dedicated to falcon-headed Haroeris (Horus in his older aspect), the right side to Sobek, the crocodile god. The two parts of the temple are only physically divided, however, at the two sanctuaries.

You enter the site past a giant ruined gateway and near it a small chapel of Hathor. If you wander into the chapel you can see that it is now used as a

Painted pillar at the Temple of Sobek and Haroeris (Horus)

display room for crocodile mummies dug up from a cemetery close by. The Nile has nibbled away at the temple terrace, causing the pylon to fall, and so you walk directly into the pronaos, its column capitals – some as lilies, some as papyrus – proclaiming the unity of Upper and Lower Egypt. On the interior wall of the façade are fine reliefs depicting various Ptolemaic kings receiving the blessings of Egypt's high gods and the double crown of the Delta and the valley.

In the hypostyle hall beyond, and in the three rising antechambers after that, are more reliefs. One, between the doors into the two sanctuaries, shows Ptolemy Philometor and his sister-wife before Sobek and Haroeris, while Khonsu, son of Amun, inscribes the king's name on a palm stalk, the equivalent of St Peter confirming entry into heaven.

The sanctuaries are badly ruined, but

they are all the more revealing for that. Between them, at a lower level, is a crypt which communicates with a chapel to the east. The crypt is now exposed but was once covered with a sliding slab. It is not difficult to imagine someone creeping down there from the chapel to make spectral noises at appropriate moments.

An inner corridor passes behind the sanctuaries and is lined by chapels in various stages of decoration. Beyond this there is an outer corridor, its walls decorated with Roman reliefs. If you face away from the sanctuaries and look just to the left of centre you will see a relief of the Roman emperor Marcus Aurelius, famous among other things as a Stoic philosopher, but here made to look for all the world like a New Kingdom pharaoh.

To his left are fascinating reliefs of medical instruments, including suction cups, scalpels, retractors, scales, lances, bone saws, chisels for surgery within the skull and dental tools – testimony to the remarkable degree of medical sophistication in Egypt nearly 2,000 years ago.

4km from Kom Ombo village, with its train station and service taxi depot. Cruise boats, however, tie up directly below the temple. Open: daily 6am–6pm. Admission charge.

The temple at Kom Ombo, dedicated to Sobek (the crocodile god) and Haroeris (Horus)

RURAL LIFE

Until the building of the High Dam at Aswan during the 1960s, the Nile annually rose and fell, inundating the surrounding countryside and then withdrawing, leaving behind a rich deposit of mud. There are still some remnants of Egypt's flood-led lifestyle. Villages of mud-brick houses still stand huddled on the low mounds which once kept them clear of the murky waters.

Age-old devices continue to be used to bring water to the fields. The simplest and most ancient of all is the *shaduf,* a bucket attached to a lever, operated by hand. The *sakiya,* introduced in Ptolemaic times, consists

of a number of buckets attached to a wheel driven by a circling donkey or ox. Also Ptolemaic is Archimedes' screw, a spiral enclosed within an inclined cylinder which raises water when it is turned.

But the ancient pattern of rural life is changing rapidly. The annual deposits

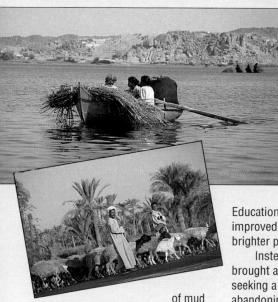

of mud have been replaced by chemical fertilisers, produced by factories operating on the hydro-electric power generated by the High Dam. Harvests have multiplied, but the fields and the river offer less nutriment now and the numbers of birds and fish are diminishing. Even the mud itself has become an unrenewable resource.

Concrete is increasingly being used instead of mud brick when building houses.

Electricity, however, has brought light to the villages at night – and television, too. The *fellahin*, Egypt's peasantry, are no longer isolated from the wider world. Electric and petrol-driven pumps are replacing the dulling labour of men and animals. Education and health care have improved. This ought to have brought brighter prospects.

Instead, improved health care has brought a population explosion. *Fellahin* seeking a better existence have been abandoning their diminishing plots in the desperate hope of a better life in the cities, which now hold half Egypt's population. Food and jobs are short. The rhythm of the past has been broken and the future is perilous.

The *fellahin*, Egypt's peasantry, depend on farming for their livelihood and agriculture remains the basis of the country's economy

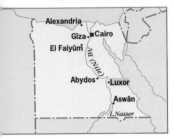

Cruising the Nile

To see Egypt from the deck of a cruise boat is one of the most pleasurable experiences of a lifetime. Although some boats cruise the Nile from Cairo to Aswân, most cruises are between Luxor and Aswân. These shorter cruises, which last anything from three to five days, often also include Dendera and Abydos to the north of Luxor.

Cruises might be in either direction, but the typical route described here is from Luxor north to Dendera and Abydos, and then south, passing Luxor, to Esna, Edfu, Kom Ombo and Aswân. If your cruise begins at Aswân, follow this summary in reverse order.

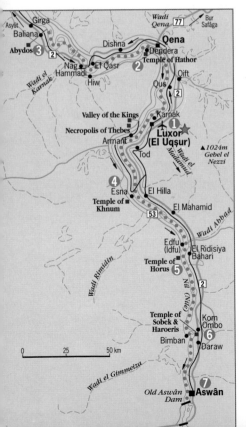

1 LUXOR

Board mid-afternoon. Tours the following day take in the Temple of Luxor and Karnak on the east bank of the Nile, and the Theban necropolis on the west bank (see pages 90–105). Sail north at evening, tying up at Dendera overnight.

2 DENDERA

Buses are on hand for your visit to the Ptolemaic Temple of Hathor at Dendera (see pages 84–5). The 1km walk along a country road leading straight to the temple is cool and beautiful, especially if it is early in the morning – try to arrange it if you can.

3 ABYDOS

Your boat may pass through the Nag Hammâdi barrage and under the railway bridge (so close a squeeze that the upper deck is cleared), to tie up off Abydos, but usually it remains at Dendera while buses transfer you to Abydos, the temple built by Seti I (see pages 82–3). You then return to Dendera by bus and sail southwards past Luxor, tying up overnight at Esna.

4 ESNA

At Esna there is a barrage, built by the British in 1906–7, which serves also as a bridge. Your boat must wait its turn to pass through the barrage by means of a lock. This happens either while you are asleep or in the morning while you are visiting the Ptolemaic Temple of Khnum (see pages 108–9). It sometimes gives you quite a bit of time to stroll about town, looking at the interesting old houses.

5 EDFU

About midday you arrive at Edfu where you are met by carriages which take you to the huge Ptolemaic Temple of Horus (see pages 106–7). Later in the day you sail south to Kom Ombo. Beyond Edfu the landscape changes, with the desert sometimes spilling down to the east bank of the Nile.

6 KOM OMBO

This double Temple of Sobek and Haroeris (Horus), also dating to the Ptolemaic period, enjoys a lovely setting on a low promontory overlooking the river (see pages 110–11). You tie up beneath it and possibly spend the night here, sailing for Aswân in the morning.

The ribbon of cultivation on either side of the river is very thin now, and often the desert presses in on both sides. South of Kom Ombo much of the local population speaks the Nubian language. You are entering another world.

7 ASWÂN

You arrive in Aswân at midday (see pages 116–125). It feels like sailing into an oasis. The town stands brightly on the east bank; a great wave of desert rises on the west. Islands, feluccas and granite outcrops seem to fill the Nile. There is something restful yet exciting about this place, as if you have finally reached the tropics.

Note that the cost of the cruise includes visits to the sites *en route*, including many of those at both Luxor and Aswân. See also page 172–3 for details of cruising.

Aswân

*T*he layer of sandstone covering Upper Egypt from Edfu southwards is ruptured here by the thrust of underlying granite which the river has sculpted into the rocks and islands of the First Cataract. Throughout history, this is where traffic on the Nile stopped, where cargoes had to be transported round the rocks. Aswân became the entrepôt for the African trade.

The sands finally close in upon the river here, and there is no more buffer of cultivation on either side. The air is hot, but also wonderfully dry, accounting for Aswân's fame as a winter resort. Though there are things to see, the town's tranquil atmosphere and the beauty of its situation is more conducive to idleness. Fortunately idleness and sightseeing can be combined by hiring a felucca and letting the breeze carry you along.

AGA KHAN'S MAUSOLEUM
See page 125.
On the west bank of the Nile, reached by felucca. Open: 9am–4.30pm. Closed: Monday. Admission charge.

The Aga Khan's mausoleum

BOTANICAL ISLAND
See page 124.
This botanical island garden, known also as Kitchener's Island, lies between Elephantine Island and the west bank of the Nile and is reached by felucca. Open: daily 8am– sunset. Admission charge.

DEIR ANBA SAMAAN
(St Simeon's Monastery)
See page 125.
On the west bank of the Nile, 2km from the river. From the felucca landing stage, you

ASWÂN

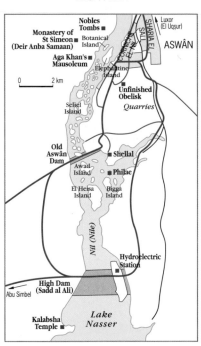

can walk across the sands in about 20 minutes or hire a camel. Open: daily 9am–4pm. Admission charge.

Elephantine Island, in the middle of the Nile, sits opposite the modern town of Aswân

ELEPHANTINE ISLAND

In ancient times the area on the east bank of the Nile, where Aswân now stands, was known as *Syene* and was famous for the nearby quarries of pink granite. Yet it was always secondary to the main commercial and administrative settlement of Yebu, which stood at the southern end of Elephantine Island. Yebu was Egyptian for elephant, while Elephantine was the later Greek name. It is likely that Yebu owed its name and much of its importance to the ivory trade.

ASWÂN MUSEUM

The displays here are all local finds, including jewellery, bronze mirrors, slate palettes for cosmetics and the statues of Yebu's governors. There is also a mummified ram within a sarcophagus, and a golden bust of Khnum, for the island was home to this ram-headed god. *Open: daily 8.30am–6pm. The admission ticket is valid also for the Yebu ruins.*

NILOMETER

This shaft cut down into the granite bluff on the east side of the island is inscribed with pharaonic, Greek, Latin and Arabic numerals. It was used for measuring the height of the Nile – and therefore the likely harvest and the tax to be imposed on farmers – from ancient times through to the 19th century.

A path from the museum runs 300m southeastwards towards a sycamore tree, where you will find the nilometer. Open: daily 8.30am–6pm. Baksheesh to keeper.

YEBU

Excavations here have revealed the remains of several temples, including the massive platform and foundation stones of a Temple of Khnum to the southwest of the Nilometer. Southwest of this, in turn, are the remains of ancient houses, the homes of the Jewish garrison posted here during the 5th century BC. At the southern tip of the island, by the water's edge, a small Ptolemaic shrine has been reconstructed.

Entry to the museum includes admission to the ruins.

Elephantine is the long palm-covered island opposite Aswân. There is a ferry to the Nubian villages. Otherwise you can hire a felucca to reach the island's antiquities.

The High Dam Circuit

*I*t is usual, when visiting the High Dam, to stop – or at least glance at – a few other places of interest along the way. Altogether, the circuit south from Aswân to the unfinished obelisk, then over the old Aswân Dam and back to the east bank via the High Dam, is about 18km. Taking a tour or hiring a taxi is the easiest option. Photography at the dams is not permitted, and it is a good idea to bring your passport for identification.

OLD ASWÂN DAM

Built between 1898 and 1902, this dam was part of a vast hydrological project undertaken by the British up and down the length of the Nile, which included barrages at Esna, Nag Hammâdi and just downriver from Cairo. The height of this dam was twice raised to increase irrigation and hydro-electric output. A road passes over the top of the dam and you can look down upon the First Cataract below, though it hardly swirls now.

ASWÂN HIGH DAM

As the population continued to grow, the old dam could no longer meet Egypt's need for new cultivatable land and increased supplies of electricity. Work began on the High Dam, 6km upstream, in the mid-1960s, and was completed in 1971. Seventeen times as much material went into its construction as was used to build the Great Pyramid of Cheops, and enough metal to build 17 Eiffel Towers. A huge artifical lake, **Lake Nasser**, reaches back 500km to the Second Cataract in the Sudan. Were the dam to break, a tidal wave would rush down the Nile valley, inundating most of Egypt's rural and urban population.

Though there are environmental drawbacks, there are also undeniable advantages. The British dam regulated the flow of the Nile during the course of a year; the High Dam can store surplus

Hydroelectric generators at the High Dam provide most of the country's electricity

Ancient remains in the desert above Aswân

have been the largest piece of stone handled in history. Work stopped after a flaw was discovered in the stone.
The ancient quarry is 2km south of Aswân.
Open: daily 6am–6pm. Admission charge.

KALABSHA TEMPLE
Rebuilt here in the 1970s, this temple's original site was 50km south, in that part of Nubia now beneath the waters of Lake Nasser. It dates from the time of Augustus and the emperor is shown making offerings to the Egyptian pantheon, for which, in real life, he had the greatest contempt.
At the western end of the High Dam.
Open: daily 6am–5pm. Admission charge.

NOBLES' TOMBS
See pages 124–5.
The tombs are on the west bank and can be reached by ferry from the northern end of the Aswân corniche or by felucca. Open: 8am–4pm daily. Admission charge.

The unfinished obelisk measures over 27m

water over a number of years, balancing low floods against high and ensuring up to three harvests a year. It has already proved its worth. During the 1980s the Nile fell to its lowest levels in 350 years, bringing drought and famine to Ethiopia and the Sudan, but Egypt was spared and millions of lives saved.

A road passes over the dam and towards its eastern end there is a viewing platform where you can gain some feeling for the size and controlled energy of the place.
The High Dam can be crossed from 7am to 5pm. There is a toll per person.

UNFINISHED OBELISK
The favoured pink granite found in ancient monuments throughout Egypt and even beyond came from Aswân, much of it from the quarry where you can still see an unfinished obelisk rooted to the bedrock. The work was undertaken during the New Kingdom, and had it been completed, it would

Philae

Completion of the British dam in 1902 submerged the island of Philae for half the year so that visitors needed to row out upon the river to look at the tops of the temple pylons and columns. In fact a sense of romance grew up around the experience. Construction of the High Dam made things worse, however, leaving Philae permanently and almost entirely drowned. The temples would not have survived many years.

The decision was taken, therefore, to transfer the monuments from the old island to another, called Agilqiyyah, which has been carved and sliced to replicate the original. The present site was opened in 1980, and with the growth of vegetation it is impossible to guess that the temples have not been standing here for 2,000 years.

Apart from the Vestibule of Nectanebos I, a pharaoh of the 30th Dynasty, the Philae monuments are Ptolemaic and Roman. There are minor temples to Harendotes and Augustus. The three principal monuments, however, are the Kiosk of Trajan, the Temple of Hathor and the Temple of Isis.

THE CULT OF ISIS

Isis, as wife of Osiris and mother of Horus, increasingly became the focus of worship. Through her suffering and her joy the goddess offered an emotive identification so powerful and satisfying that in Ptolemaic times she became identified, too, with all other goddesses of the Mediterranean world, whom she finally absorbed.

Isis was the Goddess of Ten Thousand Names, Shelter and Heaven to All Mankind, the Promise of Immortality, the Glory of Women. When all else failed, she could still save, and she was passionately worshipped by men and women alike. She was the great rival of early Christianity, which may never have given the prominence it did to the Virgin Mary but for the popularity of the Isis cult.

PHILAE

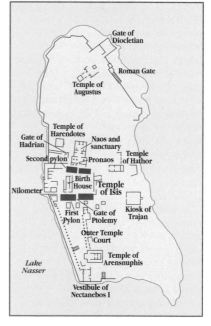

KIOSK OF TRAJAN

On the south side of the island stands this handsome but unfinished building, with 14 great columns bearing beautifully carved floral capitals. Reliefs show Trajan offering incense and wine to Isis, Osiris and Horus. The elegance of the kiosk has made it the characteristic symbol of Philae.

TEMPLE OF HATHOR

On the east side of the island, this temple was built during the Ptolemaic period but decorated under Augustus with amusing carvings of music and drinking, for Hathor was a symbol of fertility whose worship was often accompanied by merry-making. The Greeks identified her with Aphrodite, the goddess of love.

TEMPLE OF ISIS

Two great pylons lead into the temple proper. They are carved with the traditional scenes of Ptolemaic kings, attacking the enemy on the First Pylon, on the Second Pylon making offerings to Isis, Horus and Hathor. The walls of the pronaos are likewise covered with scenes of Ptolemaic kings and Roman emperors in pharaonic guise, performing the customary ceremonies. Later, when this became a church, early Christians added their crosses to the stones.

Philae, in the Nile just south of the old dam, is reached by taxi and motorboat, with many inclusive tours arranged at Aswân. The island is open daily 7am–4pm in winter; 7am–5pm in summer. Admission charge. There are nightly sound and light shows. Check for language schedules first. Admission charge.

The Temple of Isis (above) and the Temple of Hathor (below) were moved to their new site because of flooding

The three antechambers of the naos lead through to the sanctuary with a pedestal on which stood the sacred boat with the image of Isis. On the left wall is a relief of a pharaoh facing Isis whose wings protectively embrace Osiris. On the right wall, Isis enthroned suckles the infant Horus, while below that she is shown again, suckling a young pharaoh. Here her face has been gouged out by the Christians.

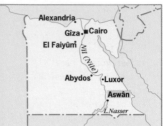

Alexandria
Gîza • Cairo
El Faiyûm
Abydos • Luxor
Aswân
L.Nasser

The Aswân Corniche and Bazaar

This walk is less a matter of seeing sights than of sensing the spirit of the place. It is best to begin an hour or more before sunset. *Allow 2 hours, though you will probably want to linger along the way.*

Begin on the Corniche el Nil, opposite the northern tip of Elephantine Island, and walk southwards.

1 CORNICHE EL NIL

There is a special fascination to the vista as you walk along the Corniche at Aswân. Instead of the usual placid cultivation, a tidal wave of desert rises on the far bank, islands force the Nile into channels, and boulders break the river's surface like gigantic bathing pachyderms. Though ugly concrete buildings line the landward side of the street, and a hotel looking more

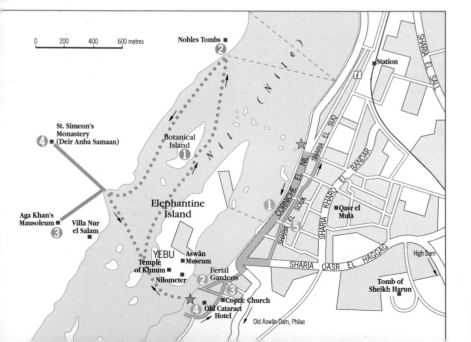

like an airport control tower disfigures the northern tip of Elephantine Island, nothing can spoil the elemental beauty of the setting.

The shrine of a local Muslim holy man sits on top of the bare hill on the west bank of the Nile, beyond the northern point of Elephantine. The row of small dark openings in the flank of the hill are the ancient tombs of Aswân's nobles.

Towards the centre of Elephantine Island are several Nubian villages, the houses painted pale yellow or brilliant blue.

The road now turns away from the Nile and begins to climb a hill.

2 FERIAL GARDENS
On your right, between the road and the Nile, are the Ferial Gardens, standing upon great loaves of granite overlooking the river. Opposite, at the southern tip of Elephantine Island, you can make out the remains of the ancient town of Yebu (see page 117).

Across the road from the gardens is a Coptic church.

3 COPTIC CHURCH
Built in 1900 to resemble a domed Coptic church, this was in fact the Anglican Church of St Mark, its font a gift of Queen Victoria of England. It has now truly become a Coptic church, to which visitors are welcome.

Continue south along the road. About 300m on, you arrive, on your right, at the entrance way to the Old Cataract Hotel.

4 OLD CATARACT HOTEL
The exterior of this 1902 russet pile featured in the film of Agatha Christie's *Death on the Nile*. If you have timed your walk well, you will have arrived here half

an hour or so before sunset. The hotel has a terrace from where, drink in hand, you can enjoy wonderful views over the Nile (see **Aswân**, page 171).

When finally the sky has gone through deepening violets to black, set off back down the hill as far as the Ferial Gardens. Instead of going along the Corniche, however, turn right into Sharia Qasr el Haggag and then take the first left into Sharia el Souk.

Souvenirs in Aswân's bazaar

5 SHARIA EL SOUK
This is the main bazaar street of Aswân, the best bazaar outside Cairo. Sensibly, in a place which is so burning hot during the day, it is only now, when the sun has set, that it becomes thronged with people.

The first 500m of Sharia el Souk retains something of the atmosphere of the old caravan days. Spices, gum and ebony out of Africa are traded here, alongside locally woven rugs and manufactured goods. Buy yourself some freshly baked flat bread along the way, and wash it down with pressed cane juice.

At any point you can turn left, walk one block, and you will be back on the Corniche.

Feluccas and Camels

From tropical gardens on Botanical Island to desert sands on the West Bank, this journey of unusual variety combines a taste of adventure with moments of sheer delight. *Allow 4 hours.*

Begin by hiring a felucca below the terrace of the Old Cataract Hotel or along the Corniche el Nil (see map on page 122).

1 BOTANICAL ISLAND

Keep an eye out for egrets and hoopoes wading among the rocks as you sail round the southern point of Elephantine Island. General Kitchener became Consul-General in Egypt in

1911, and this island was presented to him then. Here he indulged his passion for flowers, ordering plants from around the world. Now known as Botanical Island, it is pleasant to walk along its shady paths, enjoying its fragrances and the many brightly coloured birds. (See page 116.)
Sail northwards to the bare hill on the west bank of the Nile.

2 NOBLES' TOMBS

A trek up a sandy path from the landing stage brings you to a line of tombs cut into the cliff face (see page 119). They all date from the late Old Kingdom to the early Middle Kingdom and belonged to the governors, princes and priests whose lives revolved around the control of the Nubian trade. The most interesting is the tomb of Sirenput II (Tomb 31), who was a governor of Aswân during the Middle Kingdom. An undecorated pillared hall leads, by way of a corridor lined with Osiris statues, to a smaller hall, its pillars

Feluccas off Kitchener's Island

The Old Cataract Hotel was used as a backdrop for the film of Agatha Christie's *Death on the Nile*

and walls covered with paintings of Sirenput and his family. On the rear wall, Sirenput sits at a table, his son before him clutching flowers, while all around are wonderfully coloured hieroglyphics.

You now sail southwards to a cove where a path leads up to the Aga Khan Mausoleum.

3 AGA KHAN'S MAUSOLEUM

Aga Khan III lived at the white villa here, and was buried in the domed mausoleum just above it in 1957. His white Carrara marble tomb was carved carved beautifully in Cairo with geometric patterns and Koranic inscriptions (see page 116).

He was spiritual leader of the Ismailis, a Shi'ite sect, and also a man of considerable wealth and bulk. At his diamond jubilee in 1945 he was weighed against diamonds which were then distributed among his followers. His playboy son, Ali, predeceased him, and he was succeeded by his more earnest grandson Karim, Aga Khan IV.

Return to the corral near the felucca landing and hire a camel for an accompanied ride to St Simeon's. Alternatively, you can walk across the soft sand in 20 minutes.

4 ST SIMEON'S MONASTERY
(Deir Anba Samaan)

Fields and gardens once filled the desert valley leading from the Nile up to the monastery. That was until 1173, when the monks were driven out and their monastery ruined by Saladin who feared it might be used as a refuge for Christian Nubians during their forays into Egypt. Built like a fortress in the 7th century, enough survives within St Simeon's 10m-high walls to create an evocative impression of the community which once flourished here. There is a roofless basilica with badly damaged paintings of Christ and various saints in its apses. Near by rises a three-storey keep, off which were the living quarters, including a refectory, cells for 300 resident monks and dormitories for hundreds more pilgrims, as well as bakeries and workshops (see page 116).

Return to your felucca to sail back to Aswân.

For practical information on the sights see pages 116–9. Also, refer to the map on page 122.

Excursion from Aswân

ABU SIMBEL

Two temples stare out from the cliff face at Abu Simbel. On the left is the Temple of Re-Herakhte with its colossi of Ramses II, and on the right the smaller Temple of Hathor, associated with Ramses' queen, Nefertari. Before the creation of Lake Nasser, the temples overlooked a bend in the Nile and dominated the landscape. As impressive statements of Egyptian might, they served as a warning to any troublesome Nubians, while offering a welcome to peaceful traders arriving out of Africa.

Entrance to the pink sandstone temple of Queen Nefertari, wife of Ramses II

Temple of Hathor

The façade is in the form of a buttressed pylon. Between the buttresses are six colossal statues of Ramses and Nefertari. Heads of Hathor adorn the columns of the hypostyle hall inside. On the entrance wall are reliefs of Ramses slaying his enemies and a very graceful Nefertari with her arms upraised in prayer. Beyond this is the sanctuary with Hathor, as the divine cow, emerging from the rock wall. This and the façade suggest the overall symbolism of the temple, which complements that of Re-Herakhte's. There Ramses identifies himself with Horus-as-sun-god; here Nefertari is identified with Hathor, who was wetnurse and mistress to Horus as well as wife to the sun god during his day's passage and mother to his rebirth. And so, in the sanctuary, Hathor emerges as though from the world beyond where her milk brings life to the souls of the dead, while along the façade Nefertari emerges with Ramses into the morning sun.

Temple of Re-Herakhte

Arranged in pairs on either side of the entrance are the four enthroned, 20m-high colossi of Ramses, taller than the Colossi of Memnon at Thebes, wearing

Abu Simbel is 280km south of Aswân, from which it can be reached by road. Also there are flights from Aswân, Luxor and Cairo, and in 1997 the MS *Prince Abbas* will cruise between Lake Nasser and Aswân (see page 173). Open: 6am–5pm. Admission charge includes guide.

the double crown of Upper and Lower Egypt.

Osiris-type figures of Ramses stand against the piers of the hypostyle hall within. The battle of Kadesh, in which the Egyptians were nearly defeated by the Hittites, is depicted on the left, and Ramses is shown appealing to Amun. On the right, a triumphant Ramses is shown storming a Syrian fortress and capturing Hittites. In the next hall of four pillars Ramses and Nefertari are shown before the boats of Amun and Re-Herakhte. Beyond is the sanctuary, where a divinised Ramses sits with Ptah, Amun and Re-Herakhte. The temple progressively depicts Ramses, therefore, as conqueror, hero and then god.

RESCUING THE TEMPLES

Construction of the Aswân High Dam during the 1960s would have meant the drowning of the Abu Simbel temples beneath the rising waters of Lake Nasser. Instead, in an operation organised and funded by UNESCO, the temples were raised to a new and higher site near by.

However, the temples had originally been cut into a giant cliff face, and so an artifical mound had to be constructed and the temples set into it. A small doorway to the right of Re-Herakhte's temple lets you inside the air-conditioned dome. It is perhaps the strangest sight at Abu Simbel.

Colossal figures at the Temple of Ramses II

Cartouche enclosing the name of Ramses II at his temple in Abu Simbel

EGYPTOLOGY

'If you go to Thebes', Josephine is reported to have said to Napoleon, 'do send me a little obelisk.' The imperial capitals of Rome and Constantinople had long ago acquired Egyptian obelisks; and though the British drove Napoleon from Egypt before he could satisfy Josephine's desire, Mohammed Ali made good the growing appetite for Egyptian antiquities by presenting obelisks to Paris, London and New York.

That appetite was stimulated by Napoleon's invasion in 1798, when the scholars accompanying him compiled the famous *Description de l'Egypt*, the first systematic study of the country, both ancient and modern. It was also during the French occupation that the Rosetta Stone was discovered. Using its parallel Greek text as a key to its ancient Egyptian text, Champollion succeeded in deciphering hieroglyphics in the early 1820s (see page 22). Now it was possible to read the ancient Egyptians' own descriptions of their lives, their accomplishments and their beliefs.

Scholars such as the Frenchman Auguste Mariette, the German Richard Lepsius and the Englishman Sir Flinders Petrie laid the foundations for modern Egyptology. Nevertheless, throughout the 19th century the recovery of information remained secondary to the acquisition of objects. Scholars and adventurers alike freely exported almost anything they discovered, laying the basis for the great collections at the British Museum, the Louvre and elsewhere.

In 1922 all that changed with the discovery of Tutankhamun's tomb by Howard Carter and Lord Carnarvon. The spectacular find awakened an increasingly nationalist Egypt's interest in its ancient heritage. The old rule of finders-keepers was challenged, and instead of being taken abroad the treasures were put on display in Cairo.

The modern spirit is expressed by the UNESCO inscription at Abu Simbel: 'These monuments do not belong solely to the countries who hold them in trust. The whole world has the right to see them endure'.

Obelisk of Tuthmosis I, Temple of Amun, Karnak

GETTING AWAY FROM IT ALL

'The noses, ears, mouths and eyes of our party carried away enough of Egypt, which had been held suspended in the air, to found an oasis in the desert.'

WILLIAM JARVIE,
Letters Home from Egypt and Palestine, 1903–4, New York 1904

Desert Driving and Camel Trekking

'Perhaps the most wonderful part of desert life is the desert night', wrote the Egyptian explorer Ahmed Hassanein early this century. 'It is as though a man were deeply in love with a very fascinating but cruel woman. She treats him badly, and the world crumples in his hand; at night she smiles on him and the whole world is paradise.'

Paradise can in fact be approached by public transport, which follows paved roads to all the oases of the Western Desert. Hiring a vehicle, however, with or without a driver, will give you greater freedom to explore.

Some roads in remote areas, such as those between the oases of Baharîya and Farafra, and particularly between Farafra and Dakhla, can get badly potholed and sandswept, but provided your car has been well maintained, a two-wheel drive vehicle should be entirely adequate for on-road driving anywhere in Egypt. Take sensible precautions, such as taking plenty of water and petrol, travelling in pairs in remoter areas, and avoiding night driving over dodgy roads.

Off the beaten track

As soon as you get off the road, however, even just to camp overnight in the desert, you must have a four-wheel drive vehicle. Fortunately, you can sleep out beneath the stars in the must-see **White Desert**, 50km north of Farafra. White chalk formations are nightly licked into abstract sculptures by the windblown sand, and everything, both desert and sleepers alike, waken glistening in the morning as though freshly whitewashed.

Arrange things locally with Saad, of Saad's Restaurant in Farafra town. His overnight trips into the White Desert cost about LE175 per six-person jeep.

Turquoise mines

In Sinai, one of the best off-road adventures is to the **Wadi Magara turquoise mines**, which are reached by following an ancient track eastwards up the Wadi Sidri from Abu Rudeis, midway down the west coast of the peninsula. At 25km the Wadi Magara opens off to the north and it is then a short distance to the mines. They are round the final leftwards bend, 40m above the valley floor on the left.

The mines were worked as early as the First Dynasty, and as you walk deep into the valley wall you sometimes notice small turquoises, though these are of little value. If you climb higher you come to carvings on the rock face depicting Fourth- and Fifth-Dynasty pharaohs. Directly across the valley on the hill opposite are the remains of workshops, workers' houses and a fort, all pharaonic. Back down on the sandy wadi floor you can picnic beneath the shade of an acacia tree.

At the eastern end of the Wadi Sidri, head north 50km to the larger turquoise mines of **Serabit el Khadim**, where there is also a Twelfth-Dynasty sanctuary to Hathor. If you turn south at

the end of the Wadi Sidri, you almost immediately enter the broad **Wadi Moqattab**, the Valley of Inscriptions – Nabataean and Greek mostly, but also Coptic and Arabic, dating from the 1st to 6th centuries AD. Most delightful are the Nabataean depictions of camels and men on horseback carved into the valley rock. *In Cairo you can arrange four-wheel drive safaris into the Western Desert or to Sinai through Acacia Adventure Travel, 27 Sharia Libnan (tel: 3474713), or at the same address hire a four-wheel drive car from Max Rent-a-Car (tel: 3474712).*

Camels

You can also venture into the wadis of Sinai, and trek over the mountains, on camelback. Camels with guides can be hired at Dahab, Nuweiba, Na'ama Bay and Sharm el Sheikh.
Treks from one to 21 days are organised from the town of St Catherine, near the monastery, by Sheikh Moussa, office opposite the tourist centre. Charge: around LE100 per day including camel and guide.

You can hire a camel for a few hours or take a camel safari for anything up to three weeks

THE DESERT

Egypt has three deserts. Sinai and the Eastern Desert are both, for the most part, broken, mountainous areas with some vegetation in the shelter of their deeply indented valleys. Bedouin (nomadic Arab herdsmen) inhabit both these regions.

The Western Desert, an extension of the Sahara, is entirely different. Among the hottest and driest places in the world, it is a level plateau utterly without water or vegetation except where occasional springs surface at deep depressions to create oases. White sands, formed by the disintegrating rock strata, move in graceful, undulating dunes of awesome power, encroaching on fields and villages, submerging telephone poles and engulfing entire trucks. The mighty army of the 6th-century BC Persian king Cambyses was swallowed by the sands during an expedition to Siwa, and in 1805, a 2,000-strong camel caravan disappeared into the same sands.

Egypt's oases provide a valuable source of food and shelter for a wide variety of insects and birds

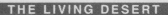

THE LIVING DESERT

Animal life is dependent on vegetation, and so only the most specialised of species can inhabit the deserts. Even these are found mostly near oases or in the northern scrubland along the Mediterranean coast. Mammals include the gazelle, desert fox, hyena, jackal and the gerbil. Migratory birds such as swallows, hoopoes, wagtails and warblers pause in the oases during their flights, attracted by the abundant insect life. Snakes and lizards are more permanent residents; indeed the Egyptian cobra, *Naja haje*, is almost an ancient monument, having served as the *uraeus* on pharaonic crowns.

The animal perhaps most associated with the desert is the camel.

Introduced from Asia, it became plentiful only during the Ptolemaic period. The ones you now see in Egypt are bred mostly in Sudan from where they are driven along the Darb el Arbain, the Forty Days' Road, from Darfur to the Tuesday morning camel market (*souk el Gamal*) at Daraw, 6km south of Kom Ombo. Others continue by train to the Friday morning camel market at the Cairo suburb of Imbaba.

Mount Sinai – sunrise from the summit (above); steps and arch on the old path up (left); pilgrims making their way down (below)

Feluccas

*I*f you have not already sailed in a felucca, you will almost certainly do so in Aswân when you visit the islands in the Nile and the sites on the west bank (see pages 124–5). You will rapidly discover you have become addicted to its pleasure, and the only cure is to have some more.

An excursion to Sehel

You could start with the half-day journey from Aswân to the island of Sehel and back. Though the current is against you as you head upstream, your boatman extends the gaff upwards, giving great height and grace to the sail, which then fills with the prevailing wind.

From the island there is a view of the rocks and swirling waters of the First Cataract, though the Nile hardly pounds and foams as once it did, before the building of the British dam. On the other hand, the ferocity of the sun as you step ashore should warn you how dangerous its rays really are, cool though you may feel as you sail along the river.

With its head into the wind, but taking advantage of the current, your felucca tacks back down the Nile. If you drink from the river, it is said, you will return to Egypt. You might have thought you would drop dead instead. In fact the Nile has a fresh and somewhat organic taste, and the boatmen drink from it all the time, saying there is no bilharzia above Esna, and certainly no danger of it from fast flowing water. On the other hand, tourists get upset stomachs, they say, from drinking ice-cold bottled water and soft drinks.

Drop out for five days

The longer felucca journey between Aswân and Luxor requires some forethought and preparation. For one thing there is the choice of blowing upstream with the wind from Luxor to Aswân, or floating downstream from Aswân to Luxor on the current. The latter is more predictable, taking five days and four nights, and it can also be a bit cheaper, costing about LE85 per person aboard an eight-passenger vessel. Stops are made at Kom Ombo, Edfu and Esna.

For an extra sum, the captain, usually an English-speaking Nubian, will also provide food, though it would probably be a good idea if you supplemented this with your own supplies. Unless you are willing to drink

---

TOURS

Agencies along the corniche at Aswân and Luxor may put together a party of six to eight people for a boat, though you are free to do that yourself. You can also decide on a shorter journey, overnight from Aswân to Kom Ombo, for example, if you are pressed for time. Find out the official rate first from the tourist office; the actual price that you finally agree with the felucca captain will depend on season (cheaper in summer) and demand generally. Payment should be made only at the end of the trip.

As an easier option, several adventure tour operators offer a felucca trip as part of their Egypt packages.

Feluccas moored up outside the Old Cataract Hotel at Aswân

from the Nile like the boatmen, also take along three litres of bottled water for each day of the journey.

You will be sleeping either on planking aboard the felucca or on the ground ashore. Nights can be chilly throughout most of the year, and downright cold during winter, so you need warm blankets or a sleeping bag. Also have a sweater for the evenings, insect repellent and, remembering how misleading the feel of the breeze can be, some form of protection – sunscreen lotion, hat, etc – against the sun, which is all the more intense for being reflected off the water.

Monasteries

*T*hroughout their long history, Egypt's monasteries have been designed for getting away from it all. It was not to escape Roman persecution that early Christians fled to the deserts, rather to escape the fleshpots of the Nile. To stay overnight at a Coptic monastery is not exactly fun, but it is certainly an escape from the 20th century.

A pilgrim's account dating from the late 4th century describes the Wadi Natrûn, known also as Scete: 'The place called Scete is set in a vast desert, and the way to it is to be found or shown by no track and no landmarks of earth, but one journeys by the signs and courses of the stars. Water is hard to find. Here are men made perfect in holiness, for so terrible a spot could be endured by none save those of austere resolve and supreme constancy'.

Demons and fables

If this is not enough to make your mouth water, consider the demons you can rid yourself of. At the Monastery of Baramous the monks exhibit a shirt

Fresco of St Paul

emblazoned with blood, its splatterings in the shape of numerous crosses. They tell you that not long ago a troubled man came to the monastery. On approaching the altar of God he shrank back in horror and in a strange voice, he cursed the monks, who anointed him with oil on his wrists and head. This caused the devil to erupt from his body, splattering the shirt with blood as he went.

It is wonderful to be a child and to be told incredible bedtime stories. It is even more wonderful to be an adult and to sit beneath a vine trellis sipping tea within ancient walls somewhere in the darkening Western Desert and to hear the incredible related from the lips of a bearded monk in a long black robe with a starry cowl pulled over his head. You are then shown to your quarters and advised to get to sleep early.

The hermits

Baramous may well be the world's oldest, indeed the world's first monastery. It is surrounded by hermits' caves for those who find even monastic life too cosy; and as you lie in bed you think of them, alone in the Western Desert, practising humility through speaking to scorpions.

One such hermit was disturbed by bursting shells and a rain of shrapnel: the Battle of El Alamein was exploding around him. A startled soldier, seeing

The Coptic Monastery of St Paul (Deir Anba Bula), south of St Anthony's (Deir Anba Antunius)

him emerge from his cave, nearly shot him dead. Even then the hermit would not move, declaring that the war was a devilish scheme to interrupt his prayers. When the smoke cleared, the British HQ in Cairo sent its apologies for the inconvenience caused.

A section for sinners

At 4am you are wakened by the sound of bells ringing through the desert air. You join the silent flow of robed figures who sweep across the moonlit courtyard of the monastery towards the ancient church. Here, amid dim candles and medieval icons, the day begins with two hours of chanting followed by three hours of liturgy in discordant Coptic and Arabic, enlivened occasionally by the tinkle of triangles.

Visitors are normally left at the outermost end of the nave, in the section reserved for sinners, where you can sleep through much of this, and even creep away altogether. For the monks, however, their devotions are followed by an eight-hour day in the surrounding fields.

In case you arrived at Baramous looking for fun, there is a notice announcing that 'Looking at the wilderness kills the lusts of the soul. Visiting the monastery should be considered a trip of rebuke and not one for pleasure.'

See page 170 for information on visiting Coptic monasteries.

Oases

*T*o the ancient Egyptians the oases were gifts not of the Nile but of the sky. As it happens, the four inner oases of the Western Desert mark the line of a prehistoric branch of the Nile and to this day feed from ancient stores of underground water.

Yet the ancients were not entirely wrong about the sky's role in creating the oases. *Wahat,* meaning cauldron, was the pharaonic name for the depressions in which the oases sit. Eroded by winds in the course of millenia, the depressions dipped down towards the water table while atmospheric pressure caused the natural springs to bubble to the surface.

And so, as you pick your way along the hot, thin line of asphalt through a landscape of lethal immensity, you can fairly imagine that these islands of fertility owe as much to the sky forces above as to the hidden waters below.

The Western Loop

A road over 1,000km in length loops far out into the Western Desert from Gîza, at first southwest to **Baharîya** and **Farafra** oases, continuing (in parts unsurfaced) southeast to **Dakhla Oasis** and then due east to **El Khârga Oasis**, finally turning northeast to join the valley of the Nile near Asyût. A new surfaced road now links El Khârga with Luxor, opening up the entire New Valley (as the governorate containing the four inner oases, but not distant Siwa, is called) to the large scale tourism already attracted to Upper Egypt.

The oases are fascinating microcosms of Egyptian rural life and history, and they can serve as bases for short trips into the surrounding desert wilderness. You can explore one or two of them in a long weekend or see them all in the course of a week's journey.

Bahariya and Farafra are the most inaccessible of the oases and so best preserve their traditional feel. The native architecture is particularly handsome at Farafra, from where also you can visit the White Desert (see page 130). Dakhla is probably the most satisfying single oasis to visit.

Date palms and gardens

The lush gardens and date groves of **Dakhla Oasis** strike a pleasing contrast with the surrounding pink and ochre rocks of the desert. It has large reserves of water, much of it brackish, and over 700 springs. At **Mut Talata**, 3km west of Dakhla's capital town of Mut, is a hot sulphur pool. Muddy brown and smelly, its effect on aching muscles is wonderful and you soon forget the aroma of rotten eggs. The best time to go is at night, when a layer of steam drifts across its surface and the sky is full of stars.

There is a lovely freshwater spring at **Bir el Gebel**, 35km west of Mut and a 5km detour off the main road to El Qasr. Here you can feel that you are getting away even from the oasis. A few palm trees sprout beside the pool which is at the foot of Dakhla's 400m-high northern escarpment. From the top there is a marvellous view. In one direction are the villages of the oasis, in the other, below the escarpment, is a field of boulders smoothed into parallel, identical teardrops by the wind.

The old part of **El Qasr**, 40km north of Mut, is an all but abandoned fortress town of towers and domes rising from a hill, though when you are in it you seem to be underground. Its alleys were covered for shade and built low and narrow to force any invaders to dismount, making them vulnerable to ambush within the maze of passages and dead ends. The thick-walled houses jut with wooden beams. The door lintels of many are single blocks of beautiful dark wood, engraved with Koranic verses. You can fully explore two of the houses which have been renovated by the Egyptian Antiquities Organisation.

Below: Brides used to take a ritual bath in Cleopatra's Spring, one of the many springs at Siwa Oasis

Red Sea Resorts

Coming to the Red Sea resorts does not necessarily mean getting away from anything. In fact it can often mean stepping into the middle of ugliness, tattiness and vulgarity. One reason for this is that most people who come are interested almost exclusively with what lies underwater, leaving developers free to ruin the landside environment.

Hurghada, on the mainland Egyptian coast 372km south of Suez, is the prime example of this. Only the big resort hotels just south of town offer relief, though if you are not a diver there is so little to do that you should not plan on staying long.

Hurghada – winter and summer resort

The best of the diving

The best stretch of coastline, both for divers and for the rest, is from **Ras Muhammad** at the southern tip of Sinai to **Taba**, 1km from the Israeli border. This is the **Gulf of Aqaba**, a northern extension of the Red Sea, rivalled only by Australia's Great Barrier Reef for the finest dive sites in the world. Its resorts are readily accessible, its sharks well fed enough to have no interest in eating you, and its landscape is beautiful.

Ras Muhammad is an undeveloped nature preserve reached only by private vehicle or boat from **Sharm el Sheikh**. People camp here, and at weekends the

place is overcrowded, yet there are no camping facilities. Sharm el Sheikh, Na'ama Bay, Dahab and Nuweiba are established holiday centres, offering camel treks, good swimming and a variety of watersports, though if you are at Sharm you must go to Na'ama Bay to hire diving equipment.

Taba

After disputing its ownership for several years, the Israelis handed Taba over to the Egyptians in 1989. The place amounts to a large luxury hotel and a tourist village. The diving here and off Pharaoh's Island opposite is interesting but unspectacular. When Saladin captured the island from the Crusaders in 1170 he built the fortress, now restored, that you see upon it today. (For more on the Red Sea resorts, see pages 74–9. For the Reefs, see pages 160–1.)

Black-spotted grunts patrol the seas

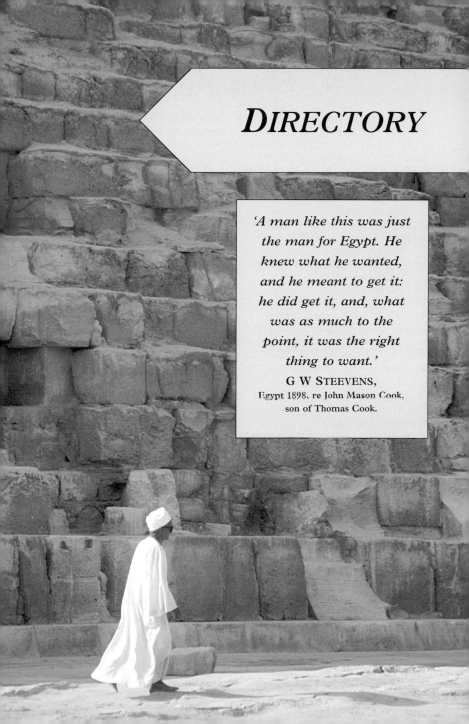

DIRECTORY

'A man like this was just the man for Egypt. He knew what he wanted, and he meant to get it: he did get it, and, what was as much to the point, it was the right thing to want.'

G W STEEVENS,
Egypt 1898, re John Mason Cook,
son of Thomas Cook.

Shopping

Simply to list Egypt's traditional crafts and wares brings to life the sights and scents of the bazaar: spices and perfumes, brass and copperware, gold and silver jewellery, glass, ceramics and precious stones, carpets, inlay work and *mashrabiyya*, cottons and leatherwork. Places like Cairo's Khan el Khalili and Aswân's Sharia el Souk are a browser's dream. There is also the chance to buy antiquities at reputable shops both in Upper Egypt and in Cairo, and antiques – *fin de siècle* to art deco – at Alexandria's Rue Attarine.

Yet the country is also moving with the times, and a new generation of craftsmen and designers is translating Egyptian themes into stylish and competitively priced clothing, jewellery, furnishings and so on, with an eye to international appeal. You will soon discover that shopping in Egypt is one of the best ways of getting to know the country.

Fixed prices

Department stores and most shops will display fixed prices. The shops in the arcades of major hotels will mark prices in Western numerals; in local shops and department stores, however, prices will be indicated in Arabic numerals, which is a good reason to become familiar with them (see page 23).

Bargaining at bazaars

You will discover that time is cheap in the bazaars of Egypt – cheap for Egyptians, if not for you. If you want to bargain well, you must be prepared to dedicate some time to it.

A stallkeeper will always ask more than he expects to get. The traditional response is to offer half as much. After several minutes, perhaps half an hour, a price midway between the extremes is agreed. That is the traditional way.

The virtue of a bazaar is that there is plenty of competition, and so, by shopping around, you ought to get a feel for price and be able to strike a good bargain. In Cairo's Khan el Khalili, for instance, you will find all the copperware in one area, all the spices in

another, all the wood and mother-of-pearl inlay in yet another. This allows you to browse around and to examine the goods, comparing styles, quality and price. It can be a good idea, also, to go to a fixed-price shop first – at least you will know the price you are out to beat.

It helps when bargaining if you appear dispassionate. The more that you show you want something the more the observant seller is likely to make you pay for it. A good technique is to bargain first over something you do *not* want and then casually to start bargaining over what you do want, almost as though you did not want anything and just bargained for the sport.

It *is* a sport and there are rules as well as tricks of the game. Your first extreme counter-offer will be laughed at and you may feel silly. Do not worry; that is only part of the game. If you feel that after several rounds of offers and counter-offers you are getting nowhere, walk out. The vendor will stop you if he thinks there is still a deal to be made. If he lets you go, you may have learnt that you are aiming at too low a price. You can still go back, or to another shop, with a better view of the item's worth.

The essence of a bargain, of course, is not to arrive at some preconceived fraction of the original asking price, but to feel that you have paid a price you could not have bettered elsewhere, a price that makes you content with your purchase and your skills.

WHAT TO BUY

ALABASTER

Vases, statuettes and reproduction antiques such as scarabs are often carved from alabaster. The best place to buy these is in shops in Luxor or workshops in the village of Gurna amid the Theban necropolis. All too frequently you will be pestered by touts offering you alabaster 'antiquities'; if you want one, offer a tenth of the asking price.

ANTIQUITIES

Any antiquities offered to you on the street are bound to be fake, which is not to say there are not genuine pharaonic, Coptic and Islamic artefacts around, although somewhat overpriced. However, it is illegal to export genuine antiquities.

BOOKS AND PRINTS

Books on Egypt and Egyptology, as well as facsimile prints of the work of such 19th-century artists as David Roberts, are available in major tourist centres throughout the country. Cairo is the place to look, however, for originals of old and rare books and prints.

BRASS AND COPPER

Brass and copper work has long been a Cairo tradition and the standard is still high today. The finest items are the big brass trays which can serve as table tops, and for which wooden stands are available. More portable items include candlesticks, lamps, mugs and pitchers, though be sure that anything you intend to drink out of is coated on the inside with another metal, like silver, as brass or copper can be highly poisonous in contact with some substances.

CAMELS

Most probably you will just want to browse and not buy at the *Souk el Gamel* in Cairo (particularly lively early Friday morning), or Daraw, near Kom Ombo in Upper Egypt, where the camels are brought for sale after being herded up from Sudan. The bargaining and trading are fascinating to watch.

Exotic Egyptian jewellery

CLOTHING AND FABRICS

The *galabiyya*, the full-length traditional garment of Egyptian men, is popular with both male and female visitors as comfortable casual wear. Fancier versions can also serve as evening wear for women. There are three basic styles: the *baladi* or peasant style, with wide sleeves and a low rounded neckline; the *saudi* style, more form-fitting, with a high-buttoned neck and cuffed sleeves; and the *efrangi* or foreign style, looking like a shirt with collar and cuffs but reaching down to the floor.

A fairly new phenomenon is designer fashion with international appeal. Prices of all clothing in Egypt will be lower than at home.

Egyptian cotton is the finest in the world, which is another good reason for buying Egyptian clothing, or having it made up for you. If you do, be warned that the workmanship is not always up to scratch and you might have to make several return journeys. You may also like to buy locally manufactured and designed fabrics to take home with you or buy cheap ready-made clothes from chains such as Octopus, Mobaco and Benetton.

GLASS

Muski glass, usually turquoise or dark brown and recognisable by its numerous air bubbles, has been handblown in Cairo for centuries. It is now turned out as ashtrays, candlesticks and glasses.

JEWELLERY

Egyptian jewellery mostly mimics the more obvious pharaonic motifs such as the scarab (for good luck), cartouche, ankh (the symbol of life) and Eye of Horus.

Items of Islamic motif show little popular imagination, the designs usually confined to hands and eyes for warding off evil or being inscribed with 'Allah'. Anything outside these two motifs is usually conceived in bad taste. The exceptions are simple turquoise strands and Bedouin silverwork. Although the range of designs is limited, gold jewellery is a very popular souvenir for many visitors.

LEATHERWORK, SHOES AND ACCESSORIES

The most common items on offer are handbags, belts, suitcases and hassocks, though Egyptian leather is not of the best quality. Also, more interesting than useful or comfortable, are camel saddles.

Shoes are possibly the major fashion retail item and range from the highly stylish to cheap and practical. They tend not to wear as well as Western-made shoes but the oriental leather slippers are an excellent buy.

MUSICAL INSTRUMENTS

Cairo is a good place to buy traditional musical instruments. These include the *oud* (lute), the *rabab* (viol), the *nai* (flute), the *kanoon* (dulcimer), the *tabla* (drum), the *mismare baladi* (oboe), and the *duf* and *riq* (forms of tambourine).

NARGILEHS

You often see men smoking the *nargileh* or 'hubbly-bubbly' at cafés. A moist lump of tobacco is put into a small terracotta cup and is kept alight by a piece of glowing charcoal. By sucking on a flexible tube, the smoke is drawn down the stem of the pipe through a container of water which reduces tar and makes for a very mild smoke. The best *nargilehs* will have glass rather than brass bodies for holding the water.

Nargilehs – just one of many interesting souvenirs on sale in the markets

PAPYRUS

The sheets of 'papyrus' sold with pharaonic scenes painted on them are often made from banana leaves. Real papyrus can withstand being crumpled up; if the one you are offered cracks when you dare to crumple it, do not buy it. You can see genuine papyrus being made at Dr Ragab's Papyrus Institutes in Cairo (see page 147) and Luxor (on a boat near the museum), and you can buy it there.

SCENTS AND SPICES

For a thousand years, Cairo has been one of the world's greatest centres for the trade in spices, which also explains its position as a purveyor of perfume essences, the aroma of history still pervading Khan el Khalili.

Egypt provides essences to many French perfumiers, who, apart from combining them in their own inimitable way, also dilute them in nostril-blasting alcohol. Egyptian perfume, on the other hand, is often made by diluting the essence in oil.

You should not count on getting quite the scent you want, as that can take some time and mixing, but the experience is fun. Essences, from musk to rose and lotus flower, are combined in the following proportions with alcohol or oil: for perfume, 1:9; for eau de toilette, 1:20; for eau de cologne, 1:30.

Cumin, sesame, saffron, cinnamon and other spices and herbs for cooking and cures, and kohl for making up the eyes, are also sold in Khan el Khalili as well as in Aswân's *souq*.

WEAVINGS, CARPETS, TENTS AND TAPESTRIES

Egypt is not particularly renowned for its carpets, but Aswân is the best place to look around for small carpets and weavings of all sorts, many of which have a bright sense of African colouring.

Tent-making, on the other hand, is a Cairene speciality, and you will often see beautiful appliqué tents used in street festivals. Decorations may be figurative, on pharaonic or Islamic themes, but the best have abstract arabesque designs or intricate calligraphy. You don't have to buy a whole tent: they are made in sections and you can buy a piece as a cushion cover.

Rural motifs and bold colours give the world-famous tapestries of Harraniyya, a village near Gîza, their naive charm. They are the creations of children who are taught traditional crafts at the Wissa Wassef Art School, which makes for an interesting visit.

WOODWORK AND INLAY

Cairene craftsmen are known for their inexpensive wooden trays, game boards and boxes intricately inlaid with mother-of-pearl and coloured bits of wood. *Mashrabiyyas*, those wonderfully carved wooden screens found in old Cairene houses, occasionally appear in the bazaars where they fetch a high price.

Where to Buy

Almost everything you might want to buy is available in Cairo, in some cases only in Cairo. Certain places may have their special attractions, the *souq* in Aswân for example, or the Rue Attarine flea market in Alexandria, but you cannot beat Cairo for its range of shops, department stores, fashionable boutiques and for its labyrinthine Khan el Khalili bazaar, with its fascinating medieval atmosphere.

In Upper Egypt and at the Red Sea resorts, a range of reputable jewellers, clothiers and the like will be found in the shopping arcades of major hotels but here, and in Alexandria, there are no shops worth singling out. Just stick to the hotels or head towards the market.

CAIRO

ANTIQUITIES
Ahmed Dahba
5 Sikket el Badestan, in the heart of Khan el Khalili.
Senouhi
5th floor, 54 Sharia Abdel Khalek Sarwat, downtown (tel: 3910955).

BOOKS AND PRINTS
American University in Cairo (AUC) Bookstore
In Hill House on the university campus, 113 Sharia Qasr el Aini, near Midan el Tahrir (tel: 3575377).
Lehnert and Landrock
44 Sharia Sherif, downtown (tel: 3927606).
L'Orientaliste
15 Sharia Qasr el Nil, downtown (tel: 5753418).

BRASS AND COPPER
The shops in the Coppersmiths' Bazaar are the places to look for brassware and copperware. You will find it at the western extremity of Khan el Khalili, along Sharia Muizz between Sharia Muski and the Madrasa of Sultan Qalaun.

CAMELS
The camel bazaar, *Souq el Gamel*, is just beyond the Imbaba district of northwest Cairo and is best reached by taxi. The market is held every Friday and starts around 6am; the activity is pretty much over by 9am. Docile females are the preferred mounts, for which you should expect to pay LE2,500.

CLOTHING AND FABRICS
Atlas
Ready-to-wear, made-to-measure and fabrics.
Sikket el Badestan, at the heart of Khan el Khalili.
George Dib
Made-to-measure clothing for men.
Semiramis Intercontinental Hotel, Corniche el Nil (tel: 3557171).
Khalil Hosney
Made-to-measure clothing for women.
2nd floor, 50 Sharia Qasr el Nil, downtown (tel: 3909270).
Nomad
Bedouin designs adapted to Western styles.
Marriott Hotel, Zamalek (tel: 3412132); 14 Sariya el Gezira, Zamalek (tel: 3411917).
Omar Effendi
Department store, good for clothing and fabrics.

Downtown branches on Sharia Talaat
Harb just off Midan el Tahrir, and on
Sharia Adli near Sharia Talaat Harb.

On Safari
Stylish clothing.
*10 Sharia Lutfalla, Zamalek
(tel: 3401909).*

World Trade Centre
A new four-storey shopping centre.
Among clothing shops here are On
Safari, Benetton and New Man.
*Just north of the 26 July Bridge at 1191
Corniche el Nil, Boulaq.*

GLASS
Sayed Abd el Raouf
8 Khan el Khalili.

JEWELLERY
Nomad
Bedouin jewellery.
*Marriott Hotel, Zamalek (tel: 3412132);
14 Saraya el Gezira (tel: 3411917).*

Saad of Egypt
Silver.
*Ramses Hilton (tel: 777444); Khan el
Khalili (tel: 921401).*

Sirgany
Gold.
*Sharia el Sagha, Khan el Khalili
(tel: 901255).*

**LEATHER, SHOES AND
ACCESSORIES**
There is a plethora of downtown shoe
shops on Sharias 26 July, Talaat Harb
and Kasr el Nil, while leather goods are
widely sold in Khan el Khalili.

Red Shoe
Fashionable women's shoes and
accessories.
Ramses Hilton (tel: 5744233).

MUSICAL INSTRUMENTS
There are several shops selling

traditional instruments on Sharia el
Qa'la between Midan Ataba and the
Islamic Art Museum.

PAPYRUS
Dr Ragab's Papyrus Institute
*On a houseboat moored south of the Giza
Sheraton (tel: 3488676).*

SCENTS AND SPICES
Khan el Khalili's spice and perfume
bazaars are in the southeast quadrant
formed by the intersection of Sharia el
Muizz and Sharia el Muski, though
spilling beyond.

**WEAVINGS, CARPETS, TENTS
AND TAPESTRIES**
The tent-makers' bazaar is on Sharia
Muizz, immediately south of Bab
Zuwayla.

Senouhi
All kinds of carpets. This is also the
exclusive outlet for Harraniyya
tapestries.
*5th floor, 54 Sharia Abdel Khalek Sarwat,
downtown (tel: 3910955).*

WOODWORK AND INLAY
Mother of Pearl Products
6 Khan el Khalili.

Entertainment

*W*ith the almost complete disappearance of its formerly cosmopolitan population since the 1950s, the range, quantity and distribution of entertainment in Egypt has become much reduced. Alexandria, once full of Greeks, Italians, Jews, English, French and others, now has virtually no nightlife or cultural activity that the passing visitor would notice. With the exception of Cairo, the same is true throughout the country, unless a luxury hotel lays on a tourist show.

In Cairo there is entertainment until the early hours, and it is a special pleasure at the end of a long night out to see the sun come up while the calls for dawn prayers echo across the city.

Many well-to-do Egyptians with Western interests attend ballet, opera and concerts at Cairo's new Opera House, and foreign cultural centres like the British Council offer various film, music and theatrical programmes. It is even possible to go tenpin bowling.

However, visitors on a short stay may not have the time or the inclination to seek these events out. Folklore entertainments are still staged, in specialist theatres and large hotels, but often more rewarding are those genuine manifestations of popular culture, the *moulids* and other festivals (see pages 154–5).

Visitors, therefore, should understand that even in Cairo the entertainments likely to attract them will be those provided at the hotels, and that outside Cairo there is virtually nowhere else to go. The monthly magazine *Egypt Today* and the weekly English-language edition of *Al Ahram* will give you a fairly good idea of what is going on.

WHAT'S ON OFFER

BARS

Almost all bars are within hotels or form part of a restaurant or nightclub. Many will have some form of entertainment. While the consumption of alcohol is legal, it is illegal to serve Egyptians (be they Copts or Muslims) during Ramadan or other festivals, which means bars not in international hotels are likely to be closed then.

CASINOS

Admission to casinos, found in many major hotels, is restricted to non-Egyptians. Play is in US dollars, with free drinks to punters. Doors close at dawn.

Traditional Egyptian entertainment

CINEMAS

English-language films are frequently shown, subtitled in Arabic. Sometimes the Egyptian audience, being able to read the subtitles, does not have to listen to the dialogue but instead chatters away, making it difficult to hear, but audiences are becoming better-behaved. Prices are very reasonable.

DISCOS

Almost all discos are at the major hotels, and many of these are restricted to guests or members. Women will usually have no trouble entering alone, but men will often find that they cannot enter without a woman. You should phone first to check.

EGYPTIAN DANCE AND MUSIC

El Jeel is the rhythmic pop music of Egypt, a blend of Nubian, Bedouin and Libyan beats. Live performances are sometimes included in nightclub programmes at Cairo's major hotels, or downtown or along the Pyramids Road. Classical Arab music is presented at Cairo's Sayed Darwish Concert Hall in Gîza, while folkloric music and dance is presented at the Balloon Theatre in the Cairo district of Agouza.

NIGHTCLUBS

The best nightclubs are found in Cairo's main international hotels. They usually offer a programme of both oriental and Western acts, for example a first-class Egyptian belly dancer between thick slices of second-rate pseudo-Las Vegas showgirl acts. A four-course dinner is served from about 8pm onwards, the belly dancer usually coming on late, at about 11pm. Reservations are required.

OPERA, BALLET AND THEATRE

The Cairo Opera House is home to the Cairo Ballet Company and the Cairo Symphony Orchestra, and is the venue for visiting operas, plays and musicals.

WHERE TO GO

As entertainments throughout most of Egypt are confined almost entirely to the tourist programmes at the major hotels, the following list deals only with Cairo where hotels comprise an important part, but not the whole, of the entertainment scene.

BARS
The Cellar
This is a meeting place for younger Cairenes.
President Hotel, 22 Sharia Taha Hussein, Zamalek (tel: 3400718).

Matchpoint
Attracts the wealthier younger set.
In the Four Corners complex, 4 Sharia Hassan Sabry, Zamalek (tel: 3412961).

Le Pacha 1901
A tied-up riverboat containing Johnny's Pub and Il Pianoforte piano bar.
Sharia Serai el Gezirah, Zamalek (tel: 3405734).

Taverne du Champ de Mars
Rebuilt from an original Brussels bar.
Nile Hilton Hotel, Midan el Tahrir (tel: 767444).

Windows on the World
Fantastic views over Cairo.
Ramses Hilton Hotel, Corniche el Nil, Boulaq (tel: 777444, ext 3215).

CASINOS
Le Casino
El Gezirah Sheraton Hotel, Zamalek (tel: 3411333).

Casino Las Vegas
Open 24 hours.
Shepheard Hotel, Corniche el Nil, Garden City (tel: 3553900).

Casino Semiramis
The newest in town.
Semiramis Intercontinental Hotel, Corniche el Nil, Garden City (tel: 3557171).

Omar Khayyam Casino
Cairo Marriott Hotel, Zamalek (tel: 3408888).

CINEMAS
Cairo's major cinemas, art deco monuments of the 1930s and '40s but now in a poor state of repair, are almost all found around Midan Talaat Harb and Midan Orabi.

The foreign cultural centres, for example the British Council, 192 Sharia el Nil, Agouza (tel: 3453281), and the American Cultural Center, 4 Sharia Ahmed Regheb, Garden City (tel: 3549601), sometimes show films, often classics.

DISCOS
Jackie's
A disco situated in the 5-star Nile Hilton Hotel.
Nile Hilton Hotel, Midan el Tahrir (tel: 765666).

Regine's
Of Paris, London and New York fame, it is located in the 5-star El Gezirah Sheraton Hotel.
El Gezirah Sheraton Hotel, Zamalek (tel: 3411555).

The Saddle
Mena House Oberoi Hotel, Pyramids Road, Gîza (tel: 3833222).

EGYPTIAN MUSIC AND DANCE
Balloon Theatre
Venue for the National Troupe and the Reda Troupe, both folk dance troupes.
Sharia 26 July at Sharia el Nil, Agouza (tel: 3477457).

Folkloric Orchestra of Egypt
Performances with traditional instruments at a variety of venues around Cairo.
Tel: 735153.

The Cairo Opera House, home to the Cairo Ballet Company and the Cairo Symphony Orchestra

Gumhuria Theatre
Venue for the Arabic Music Troupe.
12 Sharia Gumhuria, downtown
(tel: 742864).

NIGHTCLUBS
Abu Nawas
Belly dancer and singer.
Mena House Oberoi Hotel, Pyramids
Road, Giza (tel: 3833222).

Alhambra
Live entertainment.
Cairo Sheraton Hotel, Dokki
(tel: 3488600).

Arizona
If you are looking for the bottom of the
barrel, this is it: sagging bellies and other
grotesqueries.
Sharia Alfi, across the street and a bit east
of the Scheherazade.

La Belle Epoque
French flavour.
Meridien Hotel, Roda Island
(tel: 3621717).

Belvedere
Live show includes belly dancer.
Nile Hilton Hotel, Midan el Tahrir
(tel: 765666).

Haroun el Rashid
A different show every night.

Semiramis Intercontinental Hotel, Corniche
el Nil, Garden City (tel: 3557171).

El Samar
Live entertainment with belly dancer.
El Gezirah Sheraton Hotel, Zamalek
(tel: 3411555).

Scheherazade
A non-luxe belly dance place.
Sharia Alfi near Midan Orabi, downtown.

OPERA, BALLET AND THEATRE
Cairo Opera House
A newly-built, Japanese-designed
complex, which presents the ballet
season from January onwards, the opera
season from March onwards, and the
symphony orchestra season from
September through to June.
Gezira (tel: 3420603).

Gumhuria Theatre
Plays in various languages including
English, French and Arabic.
12 Sharia Gumhuria, downtown
(tel: 742864).

Wallace Theatre
English-language plays and musicals, as
well as concerts, during the academic
year from October through May.
American University in Cairo, Sharia Kasr
el Aini, off Midan el Tahrir (tel: 3542964).

POPULAR ENTERTAINMENTS

A dancing baboon, a woman breathing fire, a man staging a backstreet performance involving a snake and a guinea pig, these are among the entertainments you might come across on the streets of Cairo or Alexandria. Weddings are also a public spectacle, the parade of ululating women, tambourine-playing men, usually a belly dancer, too, preceding the bashful bride and groom – the form is similar whether along the streets of the poorer quarters or through the lobby of a luxury hotel.

You might sit at a café like **Fishawi's** in Khan el Khalili and listen to a gipsy woman singing a wailing song, or go to a low dive like the **Arizona** at the Midan Orabi end of Sharia Alfi to watch belly dancers who've seen better days. A zany finger-cymbal player is followed by a dull Lebanese riding a unicycle across a wire 2m above the stage.

What is common to all these entertainments, the puppet shows, the story tellings and the dervish hoppings that accompany every *moulid,* is the abandonment to enjoyment with which they are each equally received.

It is perhaps this playfulness, together with a flair for the melodramatic and a touch of African oomph, that makes Egyptians the leading film makers, actors, dancers and singers in the Arab world. The long-robed Kuwaitis, Saudis and Sudanese are

not in the big city to attend the El Azhar; they have come for fun. Cairo has long been the Hollywood, the La Scala, the Motown and the Las Vegas of the Middle East. Even in the warble of the *muezzins* there is a virtuosity unheard elsewhere. It can be traced back to the drones and chants of the Coptic Church, some of whose own hymns almost certainly preserve something from pharaonic worship.

Traditional music and dance are to be found in the streets as well as in the major hotels, along with more sophisticated fare

Festivals

*R*eligious festivals, both Muslim and Christian, are often times of joyful public celebration. There is usually an atmosphere of infectious hospitality and *bonhomie*, and sometimes there is entertainment in the form of music and dancing, as well as special *souqs*.

Note that almost all Muslim festivals are fixed in accordance with the 12 lunar months of the Islamic calendar which means that they do not occur at the same time each year when going by the Western solar calendar (see National Holidays, page 186).

IMPORTANT MUSLIM FESTIVALS

RAMADAN

During this month of fasting, one of the duties of all good Muslims, nothing is permitted to pass the lips between sunrise and sunset. As it happens, more food is consumed in Egypt during Ramadan than in any other month of the year, everyone more than making up at night for what they gave up during the day.

The nights, therefore, take on something of a carnival atmosphere. This can be a good time to stroll the streets, which are illuminated by coloured lanterns and thronged with animated crowds, often with singing and dancing in the squares and cafés. In Cairo it is especially worth going to the square in front of the Sayyidna Hussein Mosque in Khan el Khalili. At Luxor the festivities take place on the grass in front of the Mosque of Abu el Haggag at Luxor Temple.

Dawn prayers in Cairo during the three-day feast of Eid el Fitr

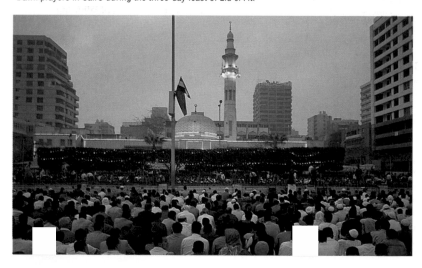

EID EL FITR

This three-day feast comes as a celebratory climax to Ramadan which it immediately follows. It is especially a time when families come together.

EID EL ADHA (QURBAN BAIRAM)

This Great Feast, which celebrates Abraham's willingness to sacrifice Isaac, occurs from the 10th to the 13th of Zoul Hagga, the month of the Pilgrimage. Everyone who can afford to will slaughter a sheep for the occasion.

RAS EL SANA EL HEGIRA

This is the Islamic New Year, which begins on the first day of the month of Moharram.

MUSLIM AND CHRISTIAN MOULIDS

A *moulid* is a festival in honour of a holy man and its devotional aspects aside it usually takes on the character of a medieval fair with popular entertainments and a *souq*.

The **Moulid el Nabi**, which is a nationwide Muslim celebration of the Prophet's birthday on the 12th day of Rabei el Awal, is marked in Cairo by a spectacular procession. As at Ramadan, the place to be is the square in front of the Sayyidna Hussein Mosque in Khan el Khalili.

Most *moulids*, however, are local affairs, albeit sometimes on a gigantic scale as at Tanta (see page 57). The **Moulid of Abu el Haggag**, whose mosque sits atop the walls of Luxor Temple, occurs on the 14th of Shaaban, and is one of the largest and wildest in Upper Egypt. During the week leading up to **St Shenute's** *moulid* on 14 July, thousands of people from all over Upper

ISLAMIC MONTHS	
Moharram	1st month (30 days)
Safar	2nd month (29 days)
Rabei el Awal	3rd month (30 days)
Rabei el Tani	4th month (29 days)
Gamad el Awal	5th month (30 days)
Gamad el Tani	6th month (29 days)
Ragab	7th month (30 days)
Shaaban	8th month (29 days)
Ramadan	9th month (30 days)
Shawal	10th month (29 days)
Zoul Qidah	11th month (30 days)
Zoul Hagga	12th month (29 days, 30 in leap years)

Egypt attend the sprawling encampment of tented stalls at the White Monastery outside Sohâg, where the night is filled with drifting laughter, the aroma of cooked foods, and the sinuous sound of Egyptian music.

WHIRLING DERVISHES

Mevlana, the 13th-century Sufi master who founded his sect of Whirling Dervishes at Konya in Turkey, has his followers in Egypt. Suspect, and indeed often banned in other Muslim countries, their intention is to achieve mystical union with God through ecstatic whirling. On Wednesdays and Saturdays from 8pm to 9pm, they whirl for tourists in Cairo, at the cultural centre inside the El Ghuri Mausoleum on Sharia Muizz.

SHAM EL NESSIM

This national holiday, with an important Coptic-pharaonic inheritance, falls on the first Monday after Coptic Easter. All Egyptians, of whatever religion, take the day off to celebrate the advent of spring, often picnicking on fish, onions and coloured eggs.

Children

*E*gyptians are extremely indulgent towards children, and you will find that they are welcomed everywhere, including hotels and restaurants, mosques and archaeological sites. It is this lack of fussiness towards children, however, that can expose a child to accident. Be alert to untended excavations and traffic, for example, and be sure that your children observe careful hygiene, and are well protected with clothing, hats and sunglasses against the sun. The better hotels can usually provide childminders, and medical services are excellent.

Children may well take more readily to the strangeness of their environment than you do, and they will probably find the dress, the scent and the bustle of the bazaar more interesting than a museum or tomb. Carriage and camel rides, and sailing in a felucca are particular favourites. Sound and light shows will be mysterious and fun. Floating and outdoor restaurants will seem novel, and certain theme eating places out by the Pyramids have been designed with children very much in mind. Additionally there are a number of attractions – pharaonic villages and the like – which are aimed especially at children.

AQUARIUM GROTTO

Marine tanks arranged along a labyrinth of passageways contain nearly 200 varieties of fascinating tropical fish and sea creatures.

Galabaya Park, Zamalek. Open: daily 8.30am–3.30pm. Admission charge.

CAIRO PUPPET THEATRE

The puppet shows, including old favourites like *Ali Baba* and *Sinbad*, are in Arabic. It hardly matters, though, as it is very easy to follow the action, and it somehow adds to the enchantment of the productions, which will appeal to adults and children alike. The season is from October through May, with nightly performances at 6.30pm, as well as Friday and Saturday shows at 11am.

Midan Ataba at the southeast end of Ezbekieh Gardens, downtown (tel: 910954).

CAIRO ZOO

An extensive and well-stocked zoo – the finest in the world when it was founded a century ago. There are marine aquaria with exotic tropical fish as well as camel rides.

Giza. Open: daily 6am–5pm. Admission charge.

COOKIE AMUSEMENT PARK

Rides and games.
*Near the Gîza Pyramids. Open: daily
3–11pm, from noon on Fridays.*

DR RAGAB'S PHARAONIC
VILLAGE

A two-hour tour takes you round a
replica temple and nobleman's villa,
and floats you along the Canal of
Mythology where you encounter the
ancient gods. Costumed Egyptians
perform appropriate priestly and
domestic tasks. There is also a
playground and a restaurant.
*Jacob Island (tel: 729053). Reached by
half-hourly boats from the Corniche el Nil,
2km south of Gîza Bridge. Open: daily
9am–9pm. Admission charge, children
under six free.*

FELFELA VILLAGE

An offshoot and expansion of the
original Felfela restaurant in central
Cairo. This rambling outdoor
entertainment complex is popular with
children, and has a restaurant,
playground, camel rides, a puppet show
and zoo, plus a programme including
acrobats, music, belly dancers and
dancing horses.
*Maryotteya Canal, Gîza (tel: 854209).
Open: daily 10am–7pm. Entertainment
from noon–6pm; daily in summer; Tuesday,
Friday, Saturday and Sunday in winter.
Admission charge.*

NATIONAL CIRCUS

A good one-ring affair with the usual
programme of animals, acrobats and
clowns.
*Next to the Balloon Theatre at Agouza, by
the 26 July Bridge (tel: 3464870). Daily
performances from 9.30pm. Admission
charge.*

SINBAD AMUSEMENT PARK

Bigger than the Cookie Amusement
Park near the Pyramids, this has bumper
cars, a small roller-coaster and other
rides.
*Near Cairo Airport. Open: daily in summer
5pm–2am, in winter daily 2pm–11pm,
except Friday when it opens at 10am.
Admission charge.*

EL URMAN GARDENS

Formerly gardens belonging to the
khedives of Egypt, they provide plenty of
space for kids to chase around or to
enjoy a picnic after a visit to the zoo.
Avoid Fridays when it gets crowded.
*Gîza, opposite Cairo Zoo. Open: daily
8am–8pm, closes Thursday at noon and
all day Friday. Admission charge.*

Sport

*A*part from the Red Sea resorts, with their almost exclusive concentration on diving activities, the main centre for sport is Cairo, which provides well for visitors wanting to keep fit or have some fun with a game of tennis or golf.

THE ALL-ROUND CHOICE

The best all-round place is the Gezira Sporting Club, the oldest and most distinguished club in Cairo. Founded in 1888, it was built primarily for the British and a select number of Egyptians and offered, then, as now, such sports as polo and croquet. With the 1952 revolution, however, most foreign members were thrown out and Egyptians were more freely admitted. Today, though it is no longer a foreign preserve, it still has more foreign members than any other club in Cairo.

The club offers 23 sports including football, gymnastics and judo, and also horse racing every Saturday and Sunday throughout the winter. Facilities include a nine-hole golf course, a running track, winter and summer swimming pools, and plenty of courts for tennis, squash, handball and volleyball. Additionally, it hires out the latest videos and shows new films once a week.

Gezira Sporting Club, Sharia Saray el Gezira, Zamalek (tel: 3402272). Open: 8am–11pm. Admission charge.

CYCLING

The **Cairo Cyclists** (tel: 3506647) meet every Friday at 8am at the front gate of the Cairo American College, 1 Midan Digla. The route, distance and pace is decided by those joining the ride. A second group devoted to fast paced training rides meets at 7am on Saturdays.

DIVING

The **Cairo Divers Group** (tel: 3400889 or 3608976) meets on the first Monday of each month at the Semiramis Intercontinental Hotel. Its more than 300 members of 11 nationalities have joined together to promote the exploration of the Red Sea, and their meetings are open to all.

GOLF

The Mena House Hotel is a well-watered oasis beneath the brow of the Pyramids. Its nine-hole course is the best in Cairo.

Pyramids Road, Giza (tel: 3415121). Admission charge.

HEALTH CLUBS

All the luxury-class hotels have health clubs, and staying at the hotel gives you automatic temporary membership. Many also admit non-residents on a daily or weekly basis.

Nile Hilton Health Club
Facilities include a gymnasium, swimming pool, tennis courts and sauna.

The waters off Hurghada offer excellent opportunities for fans of watersports

Nile Hilton Hotel, Midan el Tahrir (tel: 5780444). Open: daily 10am–10pm. Charges vary according to facility used.

Splash

Newly renovated, the facilities include a swimming pool, jacuzzi, rowing and cycling machines, floodlit tennis courts, sauna and health food bar.
Marriott Hotel, Zamalek (tel: 3408888). Open: daily 7am–10pm. Charges vary according to facility used.

RUNNING

The **Hash House Harriers** meet every Friday afternoon at about two hours before sunset for non-competitive fun runs at the Pyramids, in the desert, and through the more traffic-free parts of town. Members include people of all nationalities, ages, sexes and ability (tel: 3507183 for a recorded message).

SPECTATOR SPORTS

FOOTBALL, HORSE RACING AND ROWING

For the latest information on spectator sports, get a copy of the daily newspaper, *The Egyptian Gazette* (called *The Egyptian Mail* on Saturdays).

Egypt's favourite sport is football, the two main teams being Zamalek and Ahly. The season is from September through May, with games played on Fridays, Saturdays and Sundays at the Cairo Stadium in Heliopolis.

There is horse racing from October to May at the Gezira Sporting Club (see opposite) and the Heliopolis Hippodrome.

On Fridays year-round you can watch visiting British and American university rowing crews being thrashed on the Nile by the Cairo police crew.

RED SEA REEFS

The Red Sea offers perfect conditions for the growth of coral. As well as having a high water temperature, which in itself promotes growth, the greater part of the Red Sea is below the level of surface waves which can retard reef development. Nor do any major rivers spill into the sea, so its waters are exceptionally clear, allowing sunlight to penetrate deeply. As a result, Red Sea reefs extend deeper than in most other coral areas.

CORALS

Most visiting divers stay within the fringe reef. A shallow sandy lagoon extends from the shoreline to the reef crest, a zone often too shallow for fish to cross. It is commonly the home of organ pipe corals. Beyond this is the reef slope, which is usually very steep and occasionally overhanging, with deep caves and canyons. Here there are massive banks of mountain and staghorn corals. Further out, the fore reef now descends more gradually, almost horizontally, covered by bizarre coral reefs or pillars which can rise close to the surface.

Coral reefs constitute the most complex community of animals and plants in the sea. Many species of fish,

beyond, such as rays or lizardfish, are either protectively coloured to look like sand or actually bury themselves in it.

from jewel-like damselfish to brightly spotted snappers, make their home here, taking advantage of the abundance and variety of food organisms and the shelter the reef affords from predators, although some, such as the ferocious moray eel, do lurk in its crevices.

Adjacent seagrasses are important as a nursery ground for many reef fishes, while fish living in the sand flats

The Red Sea reefs are home to a fascinating array of marine life

Food and Drink

*F*rom simple village fare to classic Turkish cuisine, with Greek, Lebanese and French influences, Egyptian food is as varied as the country's history, geography and social structure. Most hotels in Egypt, however, cater to the tastes of foreign visitors by serving an international cuisine, so that if you want to immerse yourself in the full variety of Egyptian cooking you need to venture forth to the multitude of restaurants serving the humblest to the most exquisite meals.

VARIETY OF CHOICE

Typically, dishes will be savoury, neither too oily nor too spicy, and because only fresh ingredients will be used, the menu will vary with the season. Nubian cooking, in the south of Egypt, tends to be spicier; Alexandrian cuisine is Mediterranean. In Cairo the choice is almost limitless.

Eating places can be divided into three broad categories. There are Western-style restaurants which generally aim at a diluted or internationalised French cuisine. They will have a correspondingly wide-ranging menu. Then there are speciality restaurants – Greek, Chinese, or those pretending to be a pharaonic barge – which tend to offer one fare, with some variations and alternatives. Finally, there are Middle Eastern restaurants which run the gamut from simple Egyptian fare

Egyptian wines are readily available and reasonably priced

through to Levantine, which can be a mixture of Egyptian, Turkish, French and other cuisines. In addition, there are cafés where you can get a light meal. Wherever and whatever you decide to eat, be scrupulous about hygiene and never eat anything that has been lying around or improperly cooked or washed.

NATIONAL DISHES

Egypt's national dishes are *fool*, a paste made from the fava bean to which oil, lemon, salt and pepper are usually added. *Tamaiya* (felafel) is made from the same beans, but in this case they are pressed into a patty and fried in oil. *Tahina* is a sesame paste, while *babaganouh* is a paste made from eggplant. *Koushari* is a delicious mixture of rice, macaroni, lentils and chickpeas, topped with a spicy sauce. Meat usually comes as kebabs and *kofta*, a spicy ground meat patty.

A quiet smoke – Egyptian style

One or several of these dishes will be the entire offering of the simplest Egyptian eating places. Probably there will be no menu, but you can always go into the kitchen, have a look, a taste, and then point to what you want.

As these are national dishes, you will probably find them, even if only as hors d'oeuvres, on the menu of almost any restaurant in the country.

DRINKS

Turkish style coffee, thick and black, is ordered according to the amount of sugar: sweet (*ziyada*), medium (*mazboota*) or bitter (*saada*). Western-style brewed coffee is usually called 'French coffee', while instant coffee is almost always known as 'Nescafe' whether it is or not. Tea is generally understood as mint tea or Indian tea but usually without milk.

Western-style soft drinks, including Coca-Cola and 7-Up, are available everywhere. Egypt scores well on tropical fruit and cane juices. Tap water in the towns is heavily chlorinated, and so it is more for reasons of taste than safety that you might prefer to buy bottled mineral water. Stella beer in the green bottle can be unpredictable but is usually very good. Stella Export in the brown bottle is sweeter, more consistent, more expensive, but not as good. Egyptian wines are drinkable. *Omar Khayyam* is a dry red, *Cru des Ptolemees* a dry white, and *Rubis d'Egypte* a rosé. Imported beers, wines and spirits are very expensive. Egypt makes its own spirits, but the gin is undrinkable, the brandy compares with the Spanish variety, while *arak* (the Arab equivalent of Greek ouzo) is excellent, whether neat, on the rocks or diluted with water.

Where to Eat

In Upper Egypt and at the Red Sea resorts it is the hotels which offer not only the best but almost the only eating places that are not downright dull, indifferent and even unacceptable. In Cairo and Alexandria, however, there is a wide choice of cuisine and atmosphere.

Cairo is more expensive than Alexandria, and hotel restaurants are generally more expensive than others. The following bands give a rough indication of the cost of a full meal for one person, without alcohol:

£££ = expensive LE45–75
££ = mid-range LE30–45
£ = cheap LE10–30.

ALEXANDRIA

WESTERN STYLE FOOD
Cap d'Or ££
Art nouveau surroundings, good bar, light meals including seafood.
Sharia Adib, off Sharia Salah Salem, Mansheya (tel: 4835177).
Delta Hotel Restaurant ££
Excellent French cuisine.
14 Sharia Champollion, Mazarita (tel: 4829028).
Lord's Inn £££
Posh, romantic, and good food.
Sharia Mohammed Ahmed el Afifi, San Stefano (tel: 5865664).
Le Plat d'Or £££
Continental cuisine.
Cecil Hotel, Midan Sa'ad Zaghloul (tel: 4837173).
San Giovanni Restaurant ££
Fine view over the bay, seafood and Western menu.
205 Sharia el Geish, Stanley Bay (tel: 5467774).

Santa Lucia ££
An older popular restaurant including a good seafood menu.
40 Sharia Safiya Zaghloul (tel: 4820332).
Tikka Grill ££
The best setting in Alexandria, with marvellous views over the Eastern Harbour. The varied menu includes seafood, grills and salads.
On the seaward side of the Corniche between Midan Sa'ad Zaghloul and Abu el Abbas Mosque (tel: 805114).

SPECIALITY RESTAURANTS
Chez Gaby ££
Popular new pizza place.
22 Sharia el Horreya (tel: 4830457).

Pastroudis – one of Alexandria's institutions

New China Restaurant ££
Alexandria's sole Chinese restaurant.
Carail Hotel, 802 Sharia el Geish, Mandara (tel: 862818).

La Pizzeria £
Popular Italian restaurant, though the truth is that Egyptians are virtually incapable of making a decent pizza here or anywhere else.
14 Sharia el Horreya, near Sharia Nebi Danyal.

Rang Mahal £££
Alexandria's only Indian restaurant.
Cecil Hotel, Midan Sa'ad Zaghloul (tel: 4837173).

Sea Gull ££
Built like a castle, dedicated to seafood.
Sharia Agami, Mex (tel: 4455575).

Zephyrion ££
With its terrace overlooking the Mediterranean, this is Alexandria's most famous seafood restaurant, a Greek-run place where you choose your own fish and say how you want it done.
On the waterfront at Abu Qir (tel: 5601319).

MIDDLE EASTERN
El Ekhlaas ££
Very good oriental cuisine.
49 Sharia Safiya Zaghloul.

Hassan Bleik £
Good, simple Lebanese cooking.
12 Sharia Sa'ad Zaghloul.

CAFÉ-RESTAURANTS
Athineos £
Café, patisserie and light meals served at this one-time Greek place, ornate with columns and mirrors though overly refurbished.
Midan Ramleh, off Midan Sa'ad Zaghloul.

Pastroudis ££
Founded in 1923, this, along with the Cecil Hotel, is the Alexandrian

institution most mentioned in Lawrence Durrell's *Alexandria Quartet*. Restaurant, patisserie and indoor/outdoor café.
39 Sharia el Horreya.

Trianon ££
Indoor café, patisserie and restaurant; art nouveau décor. This was a favourite haunt of the poet Cavafy, whose office was in the building above.
Midan Sa'ad Zaghloul.

Traditional Egyptian food

ALCOHOL IN EGYPT
The consumption of alcohol is generally legal in Egypt, though an Egyptian cannot buy a drink during Ramadan, and some governorates, for example Suez, are dry all year round. Neither EgyptAir nor the railways serve alcoholic drinks, and even the international hotels will sometimes not flourish their drinks list. That being said, alcoholic drinks are readily available at hotels and most restaurants – ask and you will receive. Beer, wine and spirits are hard to find in shops. Spirits are perhaps best avoided, as there have been instances of tampering with the contents.

CAIRO

WESTERN STYLE FOOD

Le Champollion £££
Probably the best of the hotel
restaurants, the cuisine is French.
*Meridien Hotel, Roda Island
(tel: 3621717).*

La Chesa ££
Operated by Swissair Restaurants, this is
a haven of Swiss cleanliness, excellent
food and a fine cake and pastry section.
21 Sharia Adli, downtown (tel: 3939360).

Estoril £
French food in plain surroundings but
served by elaborately costumed
Nubians.
*12 Sharia Talaat Harb, downtown
(tel: 5743102).*

Justine £££
Reputed to be the best and certainly the
most expensive restaurant in Cairo, the
cuisine is nouvelle, the atmosphere
formal.
*4 Sharia Hassan Sabri, Zamalek
(tel: 3412961).*

Sheherazed £
Though neither a fancy hotel nor an
imaginatively laid-out restaurant, the
Nile views are pleasant and the food is
very good.
182 Sharia el Nil, el Aguza (tel: 3461326).

El Yotti ££
Good quality.
*44 Sharia Mohl el Din Abul Ezz,
Mohandiseen (tel: 3494944).*

SPECIALITY RESTAURANTS

Il Capo £
Casual Italian, which also does take-
aways.
*22 Sharia Taha Hussein, Zamalek
(tel: 3413870).*

The Farm ££
The speciality is roast lamb, enjoyed in a

rustic setting. The service is excellent.
*23 Maryutia Canal off Sharia el Ahram,
Giza (tel: 851870).*

Fu Ching £
One of Cairo's few Chinese restaurants,
Fu Ching's is located in a passageway
off Talaat Harb, which also does take-
aways.
28 Sharia Talaat Harb (tel: 3936184).

The Nile Pharaoh £££
A cruising restaurant which looks like a
pharaonic sailing barge. Operated by the
Oberoi Hotels group, owners of the
Mena House, there are both lunch and
dinner cruises.
*For reservations and boarding directions,
tel: 726122.*

Pizzeria ££
The atmosphere is pleasant and the food
good.
*Nile Hilton Hotel, Midan el Tahrir
(tel: 767444).*

Taj Mahal
A wide range of Indian dishes,

particularly welcome to vegetarians, with good service and atmosphere.
15 Midan Ibn Affan, Dokki (tel: 3484881).

Taverna £
Principally Cypriot, the speciality is shrimp.
3 Sharia Alfi, near Midan Orabi, downtown.

MIDDLE EASTERN RESTAURANTS
Arabesque ££
This is an elegant restaurant with a small friendly bar; adjoining it is a small gallery of work by Egyptian artists. The cuisine is Egyptian, Lebanese and Continental. Prices are moderate, but drinking imported wine will make it expensive.
6 Sharia Qasr el Nil, downtown (tel: 5747898).

Bint el Sultan ££
Excellent hors d'oeuvres, grills and desserts, all as you might find in an Egyptian home. Relaxed and friendly ambience; in good weather you can dine outside.
2 Midan Souliman Abaza, Mohandiseen (tel: 3601213).

Casino des Pigeons ££
Pigeon and chicken, grilled or stuffed, with good hors d'oeuvres and salads. The dining is outdoors among palms and papyrus.
155 Bahr el Azam, near the Giza Bridge, Giza (tel: 896299).

Felfela £
Though popular with tourists and foreign residents, it is also a favourite with Egyptians and the food is certainly good. Tree trunks serve as tables. The speciality is *fool* in all its varieties of preparation, but the menu extends to meat dishes, ice creams, etc.

15 Sharia Hoda Sharawi, just off Sharia Talaat Harb.

Nile Zamalek Hotel Restaurant ££
Evening dining is by candlelight on a terrace overlooking a huge well-kept garden. The menu is Egyptian.
Midan Sidky, Zamalek (tel: 3401846).

Odeon Palace Hotel Restaurant £
A 24-hour restaurant and bar appealing to journalists, actors, artists and tourists. The food is Egyptian.
6 Sharia Abd el Hamid Shahad, off Sharia Talaat Harb, downtown (tel: 767971).

CAFÉS
Fishawi's, Cairo's oldest teahouse, is one café you should not miss for its atmosphere of old Cairo; it is in a small alley running parallel to, but one block back from, the west side of the square in front of the Sayyidna el Hussein Mosque in Khan el Khalili.

Hotels and Cruises

*T*he number of hotels in Egypt has greatly increased over the past 10 years, though most are still in established centres and at the upper end of the market. The most rapid development has been at the Red Sea resorts. Middle category accommodation has also increased somewhat, especially in Cairo. This has taken off some pressure, but it is still a good idea to make advance reservations in Upper Egypt during the winter, in Alexandria during the summer, or if you have your heart set on a particular hotel anywhere at any time.

Reservations are best made through Thomas Cook or another good travel agent. The international chain hotels can be booked by contacting one of their hotels or reservation centres in your own country. A credit card deposit may be asked for.

Bear in mind that some areas of the country, such as the Delta, and along the Nile apart from Minya, Luxor and Aswân, will only rarely have any decent hotels. In these areas, plan your tour in terms of centres from which you can make day excursions. A Nile cruise (see pages 172–3) is another way of getting round the problem. It is usually less expensive to buy an all-inclusive package than to make your own arrangements.

Star rating

Hotels in Egypt are officially rated from five-star (luxury) to one-star. The rating system is not always evenly graduated, however, and you may find that a three-star hotel is just as good as a four-star one, or that two four-star hotels, even in the same place, vary in quality and

Amun Island Hotel, Aswân, lies across from the Old Cataract Hotel

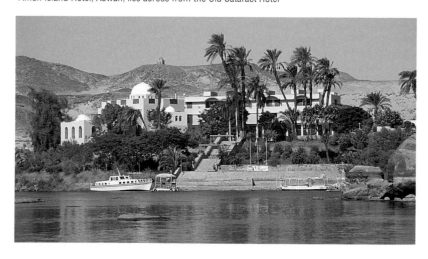

The Old National Hotel, Port Said

charge markedly different rates. As a rule of thumb, any hotel from three stars upwards will be acceptable; below that you should inspect the place and your room before committing yourself.

There are also hotels that have no star rating, and youth hostels. By and large these should be given a wide berth, though you will occasionally learn through word of mouth of some place that is acceptable.

The bill

In addition to the basic charge for a room, service charges and tax together amount to about 15 per cent. Breakfast is often an obligatory extra. Single rooms or single occupancy of a double room costs 10 to 20 per cent less than the doubles rate. Rates in Cairo are higher than elsewhere and remain the same year-round. In Alexandria and the Red Sea resorts they are about 10 per cent lower in winter; in Upper Egypt they are about 10 per cent lower in summer. Other factors affecting rates include the view and, in the lower categories, whether there is a bath in the room.

Hotel bills must be paid either in foreign currency (which can include payment by credit card at major hotels) or in Egyptian pounds accompanied by an exchange receipt from a bank. Hotels quote room rates both in US dollars and Egyptian pounds. Here they are given in dollars.

Double room rates in Cairo:
Five-star: $150–$200+
Four-star: $100–$150
Three-star: $65–$100
Two-star: $25–$65
One-star: up to $25.

Double room rates elsewhere:
Five-star: $100–$150+
Four-star: $50–$100
Three-star: $30–$50
Two-star: $15–$30
One-star: up to $15.

At Coptic monasteries there is no charge, though a donation would not go amiss. Accommodation is clean and basic. For further details on staying at Coptic monasteries, see page 179.

BOOKING INFORMATION
Hilton Hotels
UK: 99 Upper Richmond Road, London SW1G 2TG (tel: 09904 458666; toll-free 0800–894 993).
US: PO Box 11560, Carrollton, Texas 75011–5060 (toll-free 800–445 8667).
Oberoi Hotels
UK: 1 Thames Place, Lower Richmond Road, London SW15 1HF (tel: 0181–788 2070; toll-free 0800 515 517).
US: 247 3rd Avenue, New York, NY 10017–2847 (tel: (212) 752 6565).
Sheraton Hotels
UK: 210 New King's Road, London SW6 4NZ (toll-free 0800–353 535).
US: 1305 Centre Creek Drive, Austin, Texas 78754 (toll-free 800–325 3535).

Egypt's Legendary Hotels

In the pre-air-conditioned age of grand tourism, from the late 19th century to the mid-20th century, Egypt boasted a number of gloriously cavernous hotels where sunlight filtered through louvred doors and mosquito nets wavered in the evening breezes. Garden sounds and fragrances crept into the rooms, along with the occasional beetle and drift of sand. There was an atmosphere of worn elegance, though when the plaster began falling off the walls and the doors off their hinges, not even another gin was sufficient to restore the ambience for some tastes.

Too many of these wonderful old places were torn down and replaced by nondescript hotels. Some, however, have been restored and modernised without too much violence being done to their character.

CAIRO

The name **Shepheard's** conjures up visions of the past. This was the place where almost everyone who was anyone stayed in Cairo, including both General Gordon and Lord Kitchener *en route* to Khartoum. *That* Shepheard's, which was downtown near the Ezbekieh Gardens, was burnt down during the nationalist riots of 1952. Sedate and spacious though its Nileside namesake is, the present-day five-star Shepheard's was built only in 1956.

Early this century, Baedeker ranked Cairo's still miraculously standing three-star **Windsor Hotel** just below the old Shepheard's, since when it has not changed a bit. Its character is literally peeling off its walls, just as its mattresses sag heavily with the weight of history.

Even if you do not stay here, you should visit its delightful bar-cum-lounge-cum-dining room, hung with weird curios and damaged paintings, where beers are served by berobed waiters.

With the Pyramids on its doorstep, the **Mena House Hotel** enjoys one of the world's most spectacular locations. It began life as a khedival hunting lodge, becoming a hotel in 1869. This is now the old wing, magnificently decorated, where you can sit on the terrace of your suite with beautiful gardens below and exchange stares with 5,000 years of history. It was here that Churchill and Roosevelt met during World War II to initiate plans for the Allies' D-Day invasion of Normandy.

ALEXANDRIA

If you stay at the **Cecil Hotel**, make sure you have a room commanding the magnificent view over the Eastern Harbour, where the Mediterranean splashes against the Corniche. You will see the site of the Pharos on the breakwater in the distance, and off to

the right on the Silsileh headland you can imagine the palace of the Ptolemies. If that is not enough, what other hotel can say that Cleopatra put the asp to her breast just outside their front door? A Moorish pile built in 1930, the Cecil figures often in Lawrence Durrell's *Alexandria Quartet*. Ask to see the visitors' book.

LUXOR

In Luxor the heydey of early 20th-century leisured travel is represented by the up-market **Old Winter Palace**. At the rear, the rooms overlook the well-planted gardens, while the Nile flows by the carriage drive out front. King Farouk's suite was over the main entrance; you will not feel hard done by if you are given any of the other rooms gazing out towards the Theban necropolis and on to the Valley of the Kings.

ASWÂN

If you saw the film of Agatha Christie's *Death on the Nile*, you will recall Aswân's **Old Cataract Hotel**, probably the loveliest place to stay in all Egypt. Built

in 1902, it is a voluminous period delight atop a granite outcrop overlooking the southern tip of Elephantine Island. Its outstanding amenity is its terrace, an unforgettable place to sit while the sun is setting, watching feluccas flit like swallows among the rocks in the Nile below.

CAIRO
Shepheard's, Corniche el Nil (tel: 3553800).
Windsor Hotel, 19 Sharia Alfi Bey (tel: 915810).
Mena House Hotel, Sharia al-Ahram, Gîza (tel: 3833444).

ALEXANDRIA
Cecil Hotel, Midan Sa'ad Zaghoul (tel: 807055).

LUXOR
Old Winter Palace, Sharia el Nil (tel: 380422).

ASWÂN
Old Cataract Hotel, Sharia Abtal el Tahrir (tel: 316000).

Cruising

A time honoured cruise along the Nile is one of the best ways of seeing the ancient sites in Upper Egypt – a beautiful experience and the journey of a lifetime.

For the adventurous, sailing along the Nile in a felucca is the thing (see pages 134–5). If you prefer not to trust to sail and sleeping bag, there is the comfort of the traditional cruise.

A Nile cruise may form part of an overall package, or you may be an independent traveller who wants to include a cruise in your plans. It is possible to arrange both from abroad, and indeed it would be wisest if you did so. Once in Egypt you will be leaving it to the last moment and you will have to take what, if anything, is available.

Travel agencies such as Thomas Cook or the Egyptian agency Misr Travel can make the arrangements either in Egypt or abroad (see page 186). Cruise operators include Thomas Cook (see box), Eastmar, Presidential Nile, Sunboat, Abercrombie & Kent, Explore Worldwide, Kuoni and Swan Hellenic. The Hilton, Oberoi and Sheraton hotel groups also operate cruises which can be booked through their hotels or reservation centres (see box on page 169).

Prices

Prices are highest from October to May, falling by about 40 per cent in summer,

One of the many floating hotels that ply the Nile between Luxor and Aswân

and include meals, sightseeing ashore, taxes and service charges. For a five-day cruise on one of the international hotel chain boats, expect to pay about $1,500 per double cabin during high season and about $900 during low season. Local operators offer cruises at substantially lower rates.

Floating hotels

The international hotel boats, known as 'floating hotels', are the behemoths of the Nile. With 50 to 80 cabins, swimming pools, boutiques, bars, hairdressers and discos, they can leave you uncertain that you ever left dry land. You may feel that their luxury, and the number of people on board, gets in the way of the experience.

Often the smaller the boat, the better the ambience. There are several vessels of 20 to 30 cabins that are used both by local and overseas operators, and time and again it is these less prepossessing craft which win the most enthusiastic reactions from travellers.

The itinerary

There are now about 200 cruise boats on the Nile, the majority plying between Luxor and Aswân, and calling at Esna, Edfu and Kom Ombo. Some loop northwards from Luxor to visit Dendera and Abydos. Most cruises are four to eight days long, though half that time is spent moored at Luxor or Aswân while you trot round the local sites. The full cruise between Cairo and Aswân usually takes from 11 to 13 days, visiting Beni Hasan, Tell el Amarna, Abydos and Dendera, as well as the spectacular concentration of sites from Luxor to Aswân. This is a less hectic experience, which allows the Nile and life along its banks to make a profound cumulative

effect on you. All cruises include the services of an Egyptian guide who will be trained in archaeological history, but their quality can be variable. Some foreign-organised cruises will also include the services of a qualified Egyptologist who will give lectures and can answer questions. Enquire closely to ensure that your cruise provides you with the level of scholarly back-up that you want.

Traditional entertainment is a main feature of nightlife on board

THOMAS COOK NILE CRUISES

Thomas Cook invented the romantic Nile cruise, and has a range of full and short cruises on its own boats, the latest of which, MS *Prince Abbas*, begins service in June 1997. Book through any Thomas Cook travel agency worldwide, or direct from Thomas Cook Holidays, PO Box 36, Peterborough PE3 6SB, UK (tel: 01733 332255).

On Business

BUSINESS ADVICE

Volumes could be written on matters of law, finance and taxation as affecting business; suffice to say that anyone contemplating entering into a contract in Egypt, investing in the country, or establishing a business there, should first make enquiries in their home country with government departments, their bank, their legal advisor, etc, as appropriate and with the Egyptian embassy there. In Egypt they should contact the commercial affairs section of their own embassy. Most countries have embassies in Cairo and consulates in Alexandria (see page 181).

BUSINESS FACILITIES

Most Cairo five-star hotels have business centres – usually for both guests and non-guests – which provide secretarial and translation services. They will also do photocopying, send and receive faxes, etc. Many of the upper-category hotels throughout the rest of the country can at least provide you with a fax service.

Additionally, International Business Associates (IBA), offer temp secretaries, translations, professional typing and binding, photocopying, worldwide phone, fax, telex and electronic mail services, an international courier service (through Federal Express), computer support services and fully furnished business suites. They are open 24-hours at 1079 Corniche el Nil, Garden City, Cairo (tel: 3551063). Elsewhere they are open from 8am to 6pm.

281 Sharia Horreya, Sporting, Alexandria (tel: 4202312); Sharia El Finoon Madrasa, Luxor (tel: 385604); and Three Corners Village, Hurghada (tel: 447816).

BUSINESS HOURS

More westernised businesses run their working day from 9am to 5pm, but the traditional pattern, still followed by many companies, is to work from 10am to 1pm and from 4pm to 7pm. Government offices and foreign embassies will be closed on Fridays, the Muslim day of rest, and possibly Saturday. Businesses may be closed on Fridays or on Sundays, and additionally on Saturdays. Expect hours of business, or the willingness to conduct business energetically, to be reduced during the month of Ramadan.

CONFERENCE AND EXHIBITION CENTRES

All Cairo's big five-star hotels offer conference and/or exhibition facilities, with the Marriott and the Mena House Oberoi being the most popular. Large-scale exhibitions are generally held at the National Exhibition Centre on Saleh Salem (the airport road), in the Cairo suburb of Nasr City.

View from the Cairo Tower, El Gezira

CUSTOMS

Customs regulations permit the free import of all personal effects whether used or new, including such items as word processors and recorders. Nor is there any restriction on the amount of money you bring into the country. As with other visitors to Egypt, a businessman bringing in large quantities of goods or big sums of money should be sure to complete customs declarations and hold on to a copy to present if necessary on departure.

ETIQUETTE

Personal relationships are an essential part of Egyptian business life and a face-to-face discussion is always preferable to the telephone. At business meetings a suit should be worn, as casual clothing is viewed as disrespectful. Business entertainment is invariably conducted at restaurants rather than at home, and generally without the involvement of spouses. Decision-making here is a slow process. Exercise patience.

MEDIA

One initial, if somewhat thin, source of useful information is the daily English-language newspaper, *The Egyptian Gazette* (on Saturdays it is called *The Egyptian Mail*). This contains a list of all ministry telephone numbers, the daily exchange rate and gold and silver prices, as well as prayer times, and advertisements for entertainments, rentals and business services. For greater depth there is the *Al-Ahram Weekly*, an offshoot of Egypt's distinguished daily newspaper, published every Thursday in English. Its coverage includes Egyptian and Arabic affairs, the economy and investment, culture, the environment, health care, life style, sports, fashion, entertainment

and travel. The advertisements also may prove helpful. There is an occasional publication, *Business Review*, available at news-stands, which provides important phone numbers, contacts and resource lists.

To keep abreast of events generally, European newspapers are usually available in Egypt the following day, and the major international current affairs magazines are widely distributed.

RADIO AND TV

On any radio with a medium-wave band, you can tune in to the BBC World Service, which broadcasts on 639KHz from 8.45am to noon, 3pm to 5pm and from 7pm to 9pm; it also broadcasts on 1325KHz from 9pm to 3am. Five-star hotels pipe CNN and other television news services straight into your room.

Egyptian radio has 10-minute English-language news broadcasts on 95FM at 7.30am, 2.30pm and 8pm, while Egyptian television's Second Channel presents an English-language news programme from 8pm to 8.35pm.

VISAS

If you are not actually running a business within the country but are simply making a business trip, there is no reason why you should not simply state 'tourism' as your reason for visiting, in which case visa details, as set out in the **Practical Guide** (see page 176), apply.

BUSINESS HOURS
Government offices: 9am–2pm, except Friday; 10am–1pm, except Friday in Ramadan.
Private sector offices: 8.30am–1.30pm, 4.30–7pm except Friday.

Practical Guide

ARRIVING

Entry formalities

Almost all visitors to Egypt require a visa and a passport still valid for at least six months. Tourist visas can be obtained in person (usually in 24 hours) or by post (allow between four and eight weeks) from an Egyptian consulate abroad, preferably in your own country. You can also obtain a visa on arrival at Cairo Airport and at the ports of Alexandria and Port Said. Single-entry and multiple-entry (three-visit) visas each permit you to stay a maximum of one month within three months of application. You can extend your visa for a month while in Egypt. The cost of a visa will depend on your nationality and the place of application. You must register with the police within seven days of arrival. Hotels will either do this for you or tell you how to do it yourself. On escorted tours registration is normally seen to by the tour manager. Failure to register, or overstaying your visa, will result in a fine.

By air

With the exception of a few flights to Alexandria and Luxor, Cairo Airport is the point of entry for international flights. If flying EgyptAir, you arrive at Terminal One; all other airlines arrive at Terminal Two. Immigration procedure is straightforward, but queues can be long. If you do not already have a visa, go to one of the banks near the immigration barrier and purchase a visa stamp which you present together with your passport and landing card to the immigration officer. Customs inspection is usually cursory for tourists. Cairo Airport has duty-free shops on arrival and departure. (See **Customs Regulations**, page 180.)

Remember to confirm your flight 72 hours before departure. For flight information, tel: 2448566.

To and from the airport

It is possible to get a public bus (Nos 400 and 410) or a minibus (No 27) for well under LE1, taking one hour between Cairo Airport (Matar el Qahira) and Midan el Tahrir in central Cairo. It is almost infinitely preferable, however, for reasons of convenience, comfort and speed, to take a limousine or a taxi. The journey time is about half an hour. Limousines (usually large Volvos, Mercedes and Peugeots) form a rank right outside the door and will charge at least LE20 into Cairo, more towards the Pyramids. Cheaper taxis (usually beat-up smaller cars) lurk beyond; the important thing is to agree a price in advance. Returning to the airport also involves bargaining, but the price will usually be lower.

There is also a fast, comfortable and reasonably priced bus service from the airport to Alexandria. The journey takes about 3½ hours. Enquire at the Super Jet bus counter within the arrivals hall.

By sea

Ferries sail from Italy, Greece and Cyprus to Alexandria and Port Said, and also from Aqaba in Jordan to Nuweiba in Sinai. Adriatica Lines, for example, sails from Venice to Piraeus, Iraklion in Crete, and on to Alexandria, while Louis Cruise Lines sails between Limassol and Port Said.

Adriatica Lines c/o Menatours, 28 El Ghoria, El Togarieth Street, Alexandria (tel: 808407/ 806909).

Louis Cruise Lines c/o Viamare

Travel, 33 Mapesbury Road, London NW2 4HT (tel: 0181–452 8231).

By land

Several agencies in Israel offer direct coach services from Jerusalem and Tel Aviv to Sinai and Cairo.

CAMPING

The few organised campsites in Egypt are mostly along the coasts, and more often than not are without shade or adequate facilities. Some hotels provide prepared tents and camp beds. Camping on beaches can get you in trouble if you do not check with the local police first; it can also be dangerous, as some beaches are mined. Desert camping is generally less of a problem, but you should still make enquiries and attempt to obtain permission first; wells and springs, for example, almost certainly belong to someone.

CHILDREN

Children are more susceptible than adults to changes in diet, dehydration, extremes of temperature and exposure to sun, and so extra care should be taken. For general medical advice, consult your doctor well before departure.

Egyptians are very fond of children, but have a robust attitude towards them — as though they are expected not to fall down excavation pits or get run over by traffic. Do not assume that the same safety measures apply in Egypt as at home; far from it.

Small children who will not necessarily take up a seat, can travel free on buses and trains. Children under two travel free on planes and up to the age of 12 pay half fare. (See **Children**, pages 156–7.)

CLIMATE

Average temperatures in Egypt can seem surprisingly low. Cairo averages 14°C in January, 28°C in August, but these figures mask considerable extremes between night and daytime temperatures which are the result of the surrounding desert.

The coastal positions of Alexandria on the Mediterranean, and, to a lesser extent, Hurghada on the Red Sea reduce these extremes, and also give them a more even year-round temperature. As you move southwards, the air becomes drier and average temperatures increase.

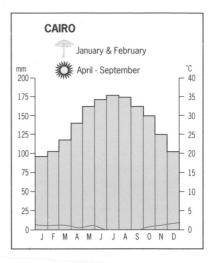

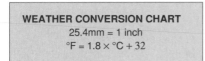

WEATHER CONVERSION CHART
25.4mm = 1 inch
°F = 1.8 × °C + 32

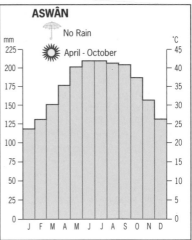

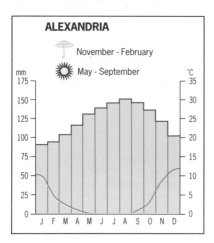

CLOTHING

In winter you will need some woollens; in summer light cottons. In spring and autumn a combination of both is advisable against warm days and cool nights. In summer at least one sweater is handy: the deserts can be cool at night, and Alexandria has strong sea breezes. Take warm clothes if planning to sleep outdoors in winter (such as on a felucca). Clothes should be light in colour to reflect the sun and be easily washable and drip-dry. Bring comfortable walking shoes. Allow for conservative standards of dress. Wear trousers rather than shorts, skirts which fall to the knee and shirts and blouses which cover the shoulders and upper arms.

CONVERSION TABLES

See opposite.

COPTIC MONASTERIES

Permission is not required to visit any monastery in Egypt. All are open to both men and women, but neither sex should wear revealing clothes. The following information applies to all Coptic monasteries:

The monasteries do not have set hours for visiting, but bearing in mind the monks' dawn and evening prayers it is best to come between 9am and 4pm.

The Coptic Church goes in for a great deal of fasting and a monastery *may* forbid entry to all or part of its enclosure during these days.To confirm details of openings you should enquire first at the **Coptic Patriarchate**, Cathedral of St Mark, 222 Sharia Ramses, Abbassia, Cairo (tel: 820681 or 831822). It would be a good idea to check with the Patriarchate first if you wish to stay overnight at a monastery, though there is a good chance of your being allowed to if you simply show up.

The Greek Orthodox St Catherine's Monastery is closed on Fridays and Sundays, but is otherwise open to visitors from 9am to 12.30pm. Staying overnight is not permitted.

CRIME

You and your possessions are generally safe in Egypt. Nevertheless, take special care with passports, tickets and money. Hotels will look after your valuables for you, but you should obtain a receipt.

Conversion Table

FROM	TO	MULTIPLY BY
Inches	Centimetres	2.54
Feet	Metres	0.3048
Yards	Metres	0.9144
Miles	Kilometres	1.6090
Acres	Hectares	0.4047
Gallons	Litres	4.5460
Ounces	Grams	28.35
Pounds	Grams	453.6
Pounds	Kilograms	0.4536
Tons	Tonnes	1.0160

To convert back, for example from centimetres to inches, divide by the number in the third column.

Men's Suits

UK	36	38	40	42	44	46	48
Rest of Europe	46	48	50	52	54	56	58
US	36	38	40	42	44	46	48

Dress Sizes

UK	8	10	12	14	16	18
France	36	38	40	42	44	46
Italy	38	40	42	44	46	48
Rest of Europe	34	36	38	40	42	44
US	6	8	10	12	14	16

Men's Shirts

UK	14	14.5	15	15.5	16	16.5	17
Rest of Europe	36	37	38	39/40	41	42	43
US	14	14.5	15	15.5	16	16.5	17

Men's Shoes

UK	7	7.5	8.5	9.5	10.5	11
Rest of Europe	41	42	43	44	45	46
US	8	8.5	9.5	10.5	11.5	12

Women's Shoes

UK	4.5	5	5.5	6	6.5	7
Rest of Europe	38	38	39	39	40	41
US	6	6.5	7	7.5	8	8.5

CUSTOMS REGULATIONS

All personal effects are exempt from duty. If you are asked to list these on a customs declaration form, make sure you leave with what you brought in, or you may be charged duty on them. If you lose anything, report it to the police and get them to give you written confirmation (you will also need this for insurance). You are also free to bring in any amount of foreign currency, but if bringing in more than US$7,000 or its equivalent, you should declare it to ensure that you can take it out again, less your reasonable expenses while in Egypt.

You are permitted to bring in three litres of spirits, plus 400 cigarettes or 250g of tobacco or 50 cigars free of duty. There are duty-free shops at Cairo Airport both before and after customs.

The export of antiquities or any item over 100 years old without a licence is forbidden.

TRAVELLERS WITH DISABILITIES

Very few concessions are made to travellers with disabilities either at museums or sites within the country or by foreign tour operators. However, the state tourist agency **Misr Travel** has a good reputation for arranging complete itineraries to suit the people with disabilities (see page 186). A person in a wheelchair could visit most temples and museums, the tomb of Ramses VI in the Valley of the Kings, and the Citadel and major mosques in Cairo. Sandy sites like Saqqâra, however, could be extremely difficult.

DRIVING

To hire a car you must have a driving licence and be between 25 and 70 years of age. Car hire is not expensive, and petrol is cheap. You can make arrangements with one of the major international companies from abroad, or choose from these and local companies when in Egypt. Hertz, Avis, Inter Rent, Europcar and Budget all have desks at Cairo Airport and offices in Cairo, and most major hotels in Cairo and Alexandria will have agency desks.

Third-party insurance is compulsory (make sure that it is included). Check that everything essential actually works (like brakes), that you have been given a spare tyre and other necessary equipment, and make a note beforehand of any dents or damage.

There are plenty of petrol stations in the cities, but they can be few and far between on the open road, so always try to keep your tank topped up.

Your main problem will be other traffic. Cairo is a madhouse on wheels, while country roads are busy with trucks, donkeys and camels. Traffic drives on the right, though you would not immediately guess it; the practice is to meander, go down one-way streets the wrong way, jump lights and so on. Avoid driving at night: vehicles do not always bother to use their lights, many have none, or beam what they have into your face.

Hiring a car with a driver will not cost much more than self-drive. Or hire a taxi for the half-day or day, agreeing the destinations and price beforehand.

DRUGS

Do not bring drugs into the country or use any while there. Possession is a serious offence, while smuggling and dealing involves mandatory sentences of either life imprisonment or death. If carrying prescribed drugs, get a doctor's letter, just in case you are stopped.

ELECTRICITY
Electrical current is 220 volts AC.
Sockets take the standard continental
European round two-pronged plug.

EMBASSIES AND CONSULATES
The following is an abbreviated list of
embassies and consulates in Cairo. A
complete list can be found in the *Cairo
A-Z* and *Cairo: A Practical Guide*, two
widely available local publications. Some
countries also maintain consulates in
Alexandria and Port Said.
Australia Cairo Plaza Tower, 1097
Corniche el Nil, Boulaq (tel: 777900).
Canada 6 Sharia Mohammed Fahmi el
Sayed, Garden City (tel: 3543110).
Ireland 3 Abu el Feda Tower, north of
the Zamalek Bridge, Zamalek (tel:
3408264).
New Zealand Consular affairs are
handled by the UK (below).
UK 7 Sharia Ahmed Raghab, Garden
City (tel: 3540850).
US 5 Sharia America Latina, Garden
City (tel: 3557371).

Egyptian embassies abroad:
Australia 1 Darwin Avenue,
Yarralumla, Canberra (tel: (062)
734437).
Canada 454 Laurier Avenue East,
Ottawa, Ontario K1P 5P4 (tel: (613)
234 4931).
UK 75 South Audley Street, London
W1Y 8EL (tel: 0171–499 2401).
US 2300 Decatur Plaza NW,
Washington DC 20008 (tel: (202) 232
5400).

EMERGENCY TELEPHONE NUMBERS
The following are Cairo telephone
numbers.
Ambulance: 123

Fire brigade: 125
Flying squad (police): 122
Tourist police: 965239 (Cairo Airport),
912644 (downtown), 904827 (Khan el
Khalili), 850259 (The Pyramids) and
753555 (Ramses Railway Station).

Thomas Cook emergency assistance
The Thomas Cook Worldwide
Customer Promise offers free emergency
assistance at any Thomas Cook Network
travel location to travellers who have
purchased their travel tickets at a
Thomas Cook location. In addition, any
MasterCard cardholder may, without
charge, use any Thomas Cook Network
location to report loss or theft of their
card and obtain an emergency card
replacement.

Report within 24 hours the loss or
theft of Thomas Cook travellers'
cheques, using their 24-hour reverse
charges telephone number: +44 733
318950 (reverse charges).

Emergency assistance can also be
obtained from the local offices of
Thomas Cook listed on page 186.

GLOSSARY

Abu: holy man or saint, whether Muslim or Christian.
Ankh: the hieroglyphic sign for life.
Bab: gate.
Bayt: house.
Cartouche: in hieroglyphics, the oval band enclosing the god's or pharaoh's name and symbolising continuity.
Copt: a Christian of the native Egyptian Church.
Corniche: seafront or riverfront road.
Deir: monastery.
Fellahin: Egyptian peasants; the singular is *fellah*.
Harem: the private family (or the women's) quarter in a house.
Hypostyle: a hypostyle hall is any chamber whose ceiling is supported by columns or pillars.
Iconostasis: in a church, the alter screen to which icons are attached.
Ka: in ancient Egypt, the spirit believed to inhabit the body during life.
Khan: an inn built around a courtyard for travelling merchants and their animals. Also called an *okel* or *wakala*.
Khedive: viceroy (Mohammed Ali and his descendants ruled Egypt as the nominal viceroys of the Ottoman sultan until World War I, whereafter they ruled as kings).
Madrasa: a mosque serving as a theological school.
Mashrabiyya: wooden screenwork, often used in windows.
Mausoleum: domed tomb chamber.
Midan: a square.
Mihrab: a mosque's wall niche indicating the direction of Mecca.
Minbar: the pulpit in a mosque.
Moulid: anniversary celebration of a Muslim or Christian holy person.
Muezzin: the person who makes the call to prayer from a minaret.

Naos: the sanctuary of a temple.
Narthex: a church's entrance vestibule.
Pylon: monumental temple gateway.
Sharia: street.

HEALTH

No inoculation or vaccination certificates are required for entry into Egypt unless you are arriving from an infected area. Your doctor, however, may recommend precautions against yellow fever, cholera, typhoid, tetanus, hepatitis A and polio. Malaria is both seasonal and regional; check before you go and if you do need a prophylaxis, take it.

Bites of all kinds need the immediate attention of a doctor. Inflammation of the eyes can be indicative of trachoma, while contact with stagnant water can cause bilharzia; the former should be dealt with immediately, the latter can await a check-up at a tropical diseases hospital at home. Do not swim in lakes, rivers or streams.

Your hotel, embassy or any pharmacist can recommend a doctor, most of whom will speak English or French. In an emergency, the following private hospitals in Cairo are best,

Pharmacy shop sign

though it is likely that a cash payment or at least deposit will be demanded: **Anglo-American Hospital**, near the Cairo Tower, Gezira (tel: 3418630). **As Salam International Hospital**, Corniche el Nil, Maadi (tel: 3638050).

You may well suffer a brief upset stomach, a normal reaction to a change of diet and climate which passes after a few days. Eat plain food and drink a lot, but if it lasts too long, consult a doctor. There is no need to stop eating Egyptian food if you feel well enough to eat at all. Your system, used to the microbes back home, will adjust to the local variety. Standard preparations for stomach upsets are available at pharmacies.

While eating in Egypt be scrupulously hygienic. Make sure your food has been properly washed and prepared. Provided even the simplest eating place has running water, there should be no problem. If in doubt avoid salads and ice-cream and stick to hot dishes. Although drinking water is heavily chlorinated and theoretically safe, stick to bottled mineral water.

Remember that the sun can be hot at any time of year, and the temperature can fall off sharply at night. During the day you should wear a head covering and sunglasses. It is not advisable to drink spirits before sundown as this causes dehydration, nor to consume iced drinks during the heat of the day. A high-screen suntan lotion is advisable, factor 6 or more. Insect repellent would be helpful.

HITCH-HIKING

You will be expected to pay for a ride. Lone women should not hitch-hike.

INSURANCE

You should take out personal travel insurance before leaving, from your travel

Hitching a free ride

agent, tour operator or insurance company. It should give adequate cover for medical expenses, loss and theft, personal liability (but liability arising from motor accidents is not usually included – see below) and cancellation expenses. Always read the conditions, any exclusions and details of cover, and check that the amount of cover is adequate.

Report any losses or thefts to the tourist police immediately and get an officially stamped statement, without which most insurance companies will refuse to pay claims money.

If you hire a car, collision insurance, often called collision damage waiver or CDW, is normally offered by the hirer, and is usually compulsory. Check with your own motor insurers before you leave, as you may be covered by your normal policy. If not, CDW is payable locally and may be as much as 50 per cent of the hiring fee. Neither CDW nor your personal travel insurance will protect you for liability arising out of an accident in a hire car, eg if you damage another vehicle or injure someone. If you are likely to hire a car, you should obtain such extra cover, preferably from your travel agent or other insurer before departure.

MEDIA

There are several English-language news and feature publications such as *The Egyptian Gazette* (called *The Egyptian Mail* on Saturdays), and the *Al-Ahram Weekly*, published every Thursday. The monthly magazine *Egypt Today* provides well-informed background features of interest to visitors and foreign residents.

MONEY MATTERS

The Egyptian pound (LE) is divided into 100 piastres (PT). Notes, being redesigned, are for 25 and 50 piastres, and one, five, 10 and 20 pounds. Remember that Egyptian currency can be difficult to convert back into foreign currency, especially outside Egypt.

Banks have exchange counters at Cairo Airport and major hotels

LANGUAGE

The language of Egypt is Arabic. Its alphabet differs from that of Western languages, making phonetic transliteration difficult. As English is taught to every schoolchild, you will probably find yourself widely understood. Nevertheless, here are some helpful basics.

Basics:

Yes	*aywa* or *nam*
No	*la*
Please	*minfadlak*
	(if addressing a man)
	minfadlike
	(if addressing a woman)
Thank you	*shukran*
No thank you	*la shukran*
Good	*kuwayyis*
Bad	*mish kuwayyis*
God willing	*inshallah*

Greetings:

Welcome	*ahlan wa sahlan*
(response)	*ahlan bik*
Hello (formal)	*assalaamu aleikum*
(response)	*wa aleikum assalaam*
Hello/goodbye (informal)	*saeeda*
Goodbye	*ma salaama*

Calendar:

Today	*innaharda*
Tomorrow	*bukra*
Yesterday	*imbarrih*
Day	*youm*
Week	*usbua*
Month	*shahr*
Year	*sana*
Sunday	*youm il ahad*
Monday	*youm il itnayn*
Tuesday	*youm it talaata*
Wednesday	*youm il arbah*
Thursday	*youm il khamees*
Friday	*youm il gumah*
Saturday	*youm is sabt*

Numbers			
0	*sifr*	13	*talatarsha*
1	*wahad*	14	*arbahtarsha*
2	*itnayn*	15	*khamastarsha*
3	*talaata*	16	*sittarsha*
4	*arbah*	17	*sabahtarsha*
5	*khamsa*	18	*tamantarsha*
6	*sitta*	19	*tisahtarsha*
7	*sabah*	20	*ahshreen*
8	*tamanya*	21	*wahad waahshreen*
9	*tesah*	30	*talaateen*
10	*ahshara*	100	*miyya*
11	*hidarsha*	500	*khamsa miyya*
12	*itnarsha*	1000	*alf*

throughout Egypt. Thomas Cook and American Express also change money.

Major brands of traveller's cheques such as Thomas Cook, denominated in sterling or US dollars, are generally accepted at exchange counters, banks, and major hotels and shops. The Thomas Cook locations listed on page 186 will cash Thomas Cook traveller's cheques free of commission. Credit and charge cards such as MasterCard, Visa and American Express are accepted at major hotels and shops. **Moneygram** is a quick international money transfer service available at all the Thomas Cook locations listed on page 186.

Banks are generally open from 8.30am–1pm Monday to Thursday and Saturday, and 10am–noon Sunday. Foreign banks may close on Sundays.

Directions:	
Where is Hotel ...?	*feyn funduk il ...?*
Where is the bank?	*feyn il bank?*
Where is the bus station?	*feyn mahattat il autobees?*
Where is the train station?	*feyn mahattat il atr?*
Where is the airport?	*feyn il mataar?*
Where is the restaurant?	*feyn matam?*
Where is the toilet?	*feyn il twalet?*
Left/right/straight ahead	*shimaal/yimeen/alatool*
Requests and shopping:	
There is/is there?	*fi/fi?*
I (do not) want	*(mish) aayiz* (if you are male);
	(mish) ayza (if you are female)
How much?	*bekaam?*
It is too expensive	*da ghaali awi*
Bigger/smaller	*akbar/asghar*
Remarks:	
I do not understand	*ana mish fahem* (if you are male);
	ana mish fahma (if you are female)
I am tired/unwell	*ana taaban* (if you are male);
	ana taabana (if you are female)
I am (not) married	*ana (mish) mitgawwiz* (if you are male);
	ana (mish) mitgawwisa (if you are female)
Go away	*imshee*
Never mind	*maalesh*
Impossible	*mish mumkin*

NATIONAL HOLIDAYS

Banks and offices will be closed on the following secular holidays.

1 January New Year's Day
25 April Liberation Day
1 May Labour Day
23 July Revolution Day
6 October Forces Day
23 October Suez Day
23 December Victory Day

Additionally, there is a plethora of religious holidays, both Islamic and Christian, which can affect days or hours of opening. The Islamic calendar is lunar-based and because its year is usually 11 days shorter than the solar Western calendar (which is used by all businesses and government departments), Islamic holidays occur about 11 days earlier each year. The most important of these holidays is Ramadan, the month of fasting, during which working hours are often shortened and effort is generally curtailed.

OPENING HOURS

Generally, department stores and shops are open from 10am to 2pm and from 5pm to 9pm or later, though in areas heavily frequented by tourists some shops may remain open throughout the day. Some shops close on Fridays, most on Sundays. During Ramadan, shop hours are likely to be from 10.30am to 3.30pm and from 8pm to 10pm or even later. For banks, see **Money Matters**, pages 184–5.

ORGANISED TOURS

Tour operators around the world offer a wide choice of package tours and cruises to Egypt, ranging from one week to one month, and including all air and ground transport, accommodation and sightseeing.

Thomas Cook, Abercrombie and Kent, Bales, Hayes & Jarvis and **Swan Hellenic** are among the leading names in tours and cruises (see page 172).

Also very helpful is the Egyptian state agency **Misr Travel**, with offices in London, New York and Sydney. Their head office in Cairo is at 1 Sharia Talaat Harb, PO Box 1000 (tel: 3930010).
Australia 630 George Street, Sydney, NSW 2000 (tel: 267 6979).
UK Rooms 201–4, Langham House, 308 Regent Street, London W1R 5AL (tel: 0171–255 1087).
US Suite 555, 630 5th Avenue, New York, NY 10111 (tel: (212) 582 9210).

Thomas Cook offices in Egypt
Alexandria 15 Midan Sa'ad Zaghloul (tel: 03 4827830). Also exchange offices at Ocean Terminal and Nouzha Airport.
Aswan 59 Abtal El Tahrir Street, Corniche el Nil (tel: 097 324011).
Cairo 17 Mahmoud Bassiuony Street (tel: 5743955); Head Office, 12 Midan El Sheikh Youssef, Garden City (tel: 3564650). Thomas Cook also have branches in Dokki, Heliopolis, Maadi and in the Semiramis Inter-Continental and Forte Grand hotels.
Hurghada 8 El Sheraton Street (tel: 065 443500).
Luxor Winter Palace Hotel, Corniche el Nil (tel: 095 372402). Also at Luxor Airport.
Port Said 43 Goumhouria Street (tel: 066 227559).
Sharm El Sheikh Gafy Mall, Gafy Land (tel: 062 601808).

PHARMACIES

Pharmacies in Egypt carry a full range of medicines, including many foreign brand names. They also often provide medicines available abroad only on

prescription. Pharmacists are highly-trained and can make helpful recommendations as to what to take. They can also refer you to well-qualified English-speaking doctors.

PHOTOGRAPHY
International brands of film are available in all tourist areas of Egypt, though while the range in print film is good, the range in transparency film is limited. Always check the 'process by' date on the film package; too often attempts are made to sell old stock. The sky and sands are bright, and much light reflects off the sea and the Nile, so slow film speeds of 64 ISO to 100 ISO will be fine for outdoor purposes.

In museums and tombs, however, where light levels are deliberately kept low and flash photography is forbidden, you will need at least 400 ISO film. Usually the fastest film available, print or transparency, is 200 ISO, though 400 ISO can often be found with some searching. If you want very fast film,

bring it from abroad. Processing labs are plentiful in Cairo and Alexandria.

Do not photograph airports, bridges, docks, railway stations, government buildings or anything else of a potentially security sensitive nature. At the very least you may find your film confiscated.

PLACES OF WORSHIP
There are Protestant, Catholic, Greek Orthodox and Coptic churches and Jewish synagogues in Cairo and Alexandria. Places of worship in Cairo:
All Saints' Cathedral (Anglican and Episcopalian), Sharia el Gezirah, Zamalek (tel: 3418391).
Church of the Holy Family (Catholic), 55 Sharia 15, Maadi (tel: 3502004).
Jewish Synagogue, Sharia Adli, downtown.

POLICE
See **Emergency Telephone Numbers**, page 181 and **Security**, page 26.

POST OFFICES
The post between Egypt and abroad can be very efficient provided you use a letter box at a major hotel or in a central location, or you go to a post office. Some letter boxes, it would seem, are visited by postal employees only very rarely, if at all. Also, anything that is not a simple letter or postcard, and which might therefore attract the curiosity of the authorities, can take a very long time to arrive.

In Cairo the Central Post Office is at Midan el Ataba, near the Ezbekieh Gardens, and is open 24 hours daily. Other post offices are open 8.30am to 3pm daily, except Fridays. Most hotels can provide you with stamps for letters and postcards.

PUBLIC TRANSPORT
Air
EgyptAir, the state airline, operates frequent daily flights between Cairo, Luxor and Aswân. With less frequency it serves Abu Simbel, Hurghada, Alexandria and El Khârga oasis (New Valley). Its private sector competitors are **Air Sinai,** which serves Cairo, Hurghada and, in Sinai, El Tor, Sharm el Sheikh and St Catherine's; and **ZAS,** which serves Cairo, Luxor, Aswân, Hurghada and St Catherine's.

Always try to make reservations, especially to Upper Egypt and St Catherine's, as far in advance as possible.

Bus
Long distance buses can be fast, cheap and comfortable. Bookings must be made in person at the relevant terminal, which in Cairo are:
To Alexandria: Superjet service from Cairo Airport, Midan Isamailia in Heliopolis, Midan el Tahrir near the Nile Hilton and Midan Gîza near the Cairo Sheraton.
To Alexandria and Mersa Matruh: West Delta Bus Company, Midan el Tahrir.
To the Delta and Canal towns: East Delta Bus Company, El Kulali terminal near Midan Ramses.
To Upper Egypt, the Faiyûm and the Red Sea: Upper Egyptian Bus Company, Ahmed Helmi terminal near Midan Ramses.
To the Inner Oases: Upper Egyptian Bus Company, El Azhar terminal, 45 Sharia El Azhar at Sharia Port Said.
To Sinai: East Delta Bus Company, Sinai terminal, Abbassia, 2.5km east of Midan Ramses.

Rail
Ramses Station (Mahattat Ramses), Midan Ramses, is Cairo's main train station. From here there are comfortable first- and second-class trains north into the Delta and Alexandria, and south into Upper Egypt, and overnight Wagons-Lits sleepers to Upper Egypt. The fastest trains take 2½ hours to Alexandria; 11 hours to Luxor; and 16 hours to Aswân. Be sure they are air-conditioned. Full timetable details are in the *Thomas Cook Overseas Timetable* (published bi-monthly, obtainable from UK branches of Thomas Cook).

For Upper Egypt you should book a day in advance; for Wagons-Lits a week in advance. All services must be booked personally at Ramses Station, except that Wagons-Lits can also be booked at **Compagnie International des Wagons-Lits,** 48 Sharia Gîza (tel: 3487354).

The railway station at Qena

Local Transport

City buses in Cairo and also trams in Alexandria are generally to be avoided as they are almost always jammed solid with people.

Taxis are inexpensive. Rarely will one operate on a meter, and drivers will usually ask for LE10 from a foreigner for almost any journey in Cairo or Alexandria. In fact LE5 will be sufficient in all cases. Carriages are a pleasant alternative, especially in Alexandria and Luxor, but they tend to cost more than taxis.

STUDENT AND YOUTH TRAVEL

Museums and sites usually offer a 50 per cent discount to students. Some discount is available on travel within Egypt, though it is limited. Youth hostels should generally be avoided.

TELEPHONES

Local and international telephone services are available in most hotels. Local calls can also be made from some kiosks, shops and restaurants. International calls can be made from PTT offices. In Cairo there is a 24-hour PTT office in Midan el Tahrir. Normally you pay first for a fixed number of minutes.
For assistance, dial 10.

International dialling codes include:
Australia: 61
Canada: 1
Ireland: 353
New Zealand: 64
UK: 44
USA: 1

TIME

Egypt is two hours ahead of Greenwich Mean Time.

TIPPING

Everyone expects something for nothing. See ***Baksheesh***, page 20.

TOILETS

Apart from the better hotels and restaurants, toilets – whether or not they are the stand-up, hole-in-the-ground type – are disgusting. Never count on there being toilet paper. Squirters are sometimes provided, or a bucket of water with which you are expected to splash yourself.

TOURIST OFFICES

In **Cairo** there are Tourist Information Offices at Cairo Airport (tel: 2454400), at the downtown head office, 5 Sharia Adli (tel: 3913454) and at the Pyramids (tel: 3850259). They can provide brochures, a good free map of Cairo, and information on accommodation, schedules, fares, etc.

In **Alexandria** the Tourist Information Office is in Midan Sa'ad Zaghloul (tel: 4807611). In both **Luxor** and **Aswân** the Tourist Offices are centrally located on the corniche.

Egyptian Tourist Offices
UK Egyptian State Tourist Office, 168 Piccadilly, London W1V 9DE (tel: 0171–493 5282).
US 630 5th Avenue, New York, NY 10111 (tel: (212) 332 2570).

ACKNOWLEDGEMENTS
The Automobile Association wishes to thank the following organisations, libraries and photographers for their assistance in the preparation of this book.
AIRTOURS PLC 140a, 159
AXIOM PHOTOGRAPHIC AGENCY 102
MICHAEL HAAG 57
NATURE PHOTOGRAPHERS LTD (D A SMITH) 140b, 160a, 160b, 161a, 161b
CHRISTINE OSBORNE 28, 99, 152, 153a, 153b, 153c, 154
REX FEATURES LTD 15
SPECTRUM COLOUR LIBRARY 156, 157
ZEFA PICTURES 14, 55
The remaining photographs are held in the AA PHOTO LIBRARY and were taken by Rick Strange, except for page 16 which was taken by Chris Coe. Rick Strange would like to thank WINGS TOURS & NILE CRUISES for their help.

CONTRIBUTORS   **Series adviser:** Melissa Shales   **Copy editor:** Melissa Shales
                    Thanks also to Michael Haag for his updating work on this revised edition